A PRACTICAL GUIDE TO
Planning & Creating a
BEAUTIFUL GARDEN

A PRACTICAL GUIDE TO

Planning & Creating a

BEAUTIFUL GARDEN

||·PARRAGON·||

Introduction

Planning a new garden and selecting and positioning plants are part of a major undertaking and are tasks that should not be hurried. It is best to begin designing a new garden by sketching a plan of the garden, showing existing features such as buildings, trees, slopes and boundaries, on graph paper. This will enable you to integrate any new features, like a summer house, herbaceous border, ornamental pond or a rock garden, successfully.

Lawns are important, unifying the entire garden and creating a foil for border plants and specimen trees. Their shape can be used to the gardener's advantage, directing attention towards a special feature, a flowering cherry tree in spring or a deciduous tree rich in colour in autumn, for example.

Choosing plants which create strong colour contrasts or delicate harmonies can be a way to personalise your garden. Different colour schemes can be used to create different effects. White flowers and foliage, for example, give a feeling of coolness in warm climates, while yellow flowers can be used to bring vitality to gardens in cooler climates.

Styles of garden vary greatly. A formal garden is certainly not to everyone's taste and many people prefer the simple elegance of a gravel garden or the more casual planting of a cottage garden, where a wide variety of plants are grown cheek-by-jowl.

No garden, no matter how well it is planned and planted, can look its best without proper maintenance. A knowledge of how the soil can be improved by adding composts and other soil improvers and an understanding of how diseases in plants can be prevented and pests controlled is essential if you are to create an attractive, lasting garden.

© Marshall Cavendish 1995

Some of this material has previously appeared in the
Marshall Cavendish partwork **My Garden**.

CLB 4380

This edition published 1995 by Parragon Book Services Ltd
Unit 13-17 Avonbridge Trading Estate, Atlantic Road
Avonmouth, Bristol BS11 9QD.

ISBN 1-85813-812-4
Printed in Hong Kong

Contents

Planning Your Garden
page 6

How to Implement Your Plans
page 12

Landscaping Small Gardens
page 18

A Lawn From Seeds
page 24

A Touch of Formality
page 30

Creating Knot Gardens
page 36

Simple Topiary
page 42

The Cottage Garden
page 48

Harmonizing Yellows and Blues
page 53

All-white Borders
page 58

Perfect Pastel Shades
page 64

Improving Soil with Compost
page 70

Home-made Compost
page 6

Using Fertilizers
page 78

Controlling Pests
page 82

Dealing With Plant Diseases
page 88

Index   *page 94*

Planning Your Garden

Planning a garden accurately on paper ensures that you get the very most from it. All the elements that you require, be they existing or completely new features, can be included on the plan, showing what you are working towards.

When changing an established garden, you must first decide what to keep. Shrubs and trees that screen off neighbours are worth retaining, but you may want to lay a new lawn, patio and path (above).

Whether you have a brand new plot with nothing in it, or an established garden, the first step is to measure up the site and draw an accurate scale plan of it.

If the garden is already established you will have to decide which features you want to retain. Incorporate these on the plan. Do not go into fine details, such as all the plants in beds or borders – just outline the planted areas.

All important permanent features should be included, such as paths, lawn, patio, garden shed, trees and large specimen shrubs.

Anything not required and that is to be cleared away should not be included on the scale plan.

An established garden may

already have a number of features that you want. With a brand new plot you can plan from scratch and this is perhaps more exciting.

Principles of design

Some features are common to virtually all gardens, so let us consider these in some detail, starting with a few simple design principles.

To create an effect of distance have at least one focal point at the end of a view. This could be a tree, a specimen shrub, a seat, a statue or a sundial to draw the eye.

If the garden is long then divide it into several self-contained areas, but still aim for some long views.

Small rectangular gardens can be made to look larger by having curved lawns and borders. Circular lawns spanning a plot help to create the impression of width in long narrow gardens.

Try to have at least one hidden area with a path disappearing into it. This could be

Don Wildridge

created with a trellis or fencing screen, a screen-block wall or a hedge.

Such an area helps to create an element of surprise in a garden, and should be attempted even in the smallest plot. Even something as simple as a small seat placed behind a group of tallish shrubs will give you a secluded, 'secret' area for sitting quietly.

Traditionally, vegetable and fruit plots are sited at the end of a garden, but if you have a large plot it may be more sen-

Circular lawns (above) create an illusion of width in a narrow garden. The central birdbath catches the eye and is a focal point.

MEASURING THE SITE

The plot and house have to be measured up and transferred to paper.

You should start by measuring the outside perimeter of the house and transferring this to the graph paper.

But first you will need some simple equipment, including a strong tape measure (a steel tape is probably best); several long lengths of cord or nylon; some pointed wooden stakes about 30cm/ 12in in length; some 1.2m/4ft long bamboo canes; and a large right-angle triangle made of three lengths of wood (the formula for making this is three, four, five).

Establish a base line from which to measure. Generally, the most convenient is the wall of the house that faces the largest part of the garden.

Working from this wall, run lines (which can be marked with canes) at right angles to it until they meet the boundary of the plot.

If the sight line is interrupted, say by shrubs or other plants, then insert canes along the line. Each cane must be exactly in front of the preceding one when viewed with the eye close to it.

These lines are measured and then transferred to the graph paper. The boundary points can be marked on the paper with dots.

Then from points along these first lines you can run 'branch lines', at right angles, to other parts of the boundary. Measure these distances and transfer them to the plan.

When a garden is all round a house, or on

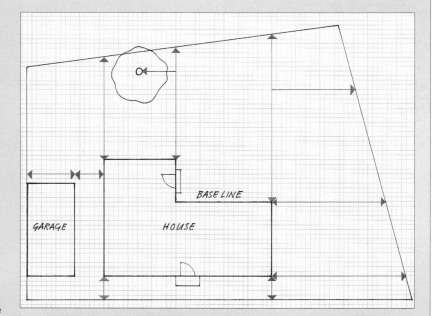

several sides of it, the other house walls must be used as further base lines to make more right-angle measurements.

When all necessary dots have been made on your graph paper you can join them up to outline the perimeter of the plot.

Then, from the base lines, measure in a similar way to any other permanent features that will be retained. Include these on your plan.

Take right-angle measurements to establish your boundaries. The scale here is 1 inch to 10 feet but the illustration has been reduced down.

DRAWING A GARDEN PLAN

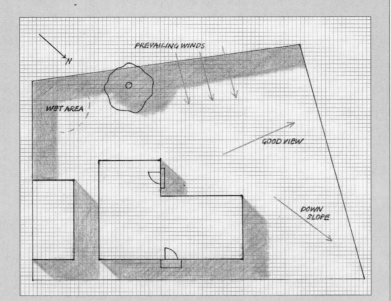

You will need to draw a scale plan of your plot, showing the house and garden. This is best done on graph paper, using a soft pencil so that you can easily erase any mistakes you make.

The larger the paper the better, as the easier it will be to draw a really accurate plan of the whole site.

You should choose a scale that will enable the entire plot to be drawn on one sheet of graph paper. Convenient scales are 1.2m or 2.4m to 2.5cm (about 4ft or 8ft to 1in), but on graph paper with one-inch squares that are divided into tenths it makes sense to use a scale of 10ft to 1in. (approximately 3m to 2.5cm).

Firstly, draw the perimeter plan on the paper, together with the house and any permanent features that are to be retained, including trees and outbuildings.

Then clip a sheet of tracing paper over the graph paper to draw in other features. These can include slopes and mounds, good views, eyesores, the direction of the prevailing wind, suntraps, boggy areas and so on.

Another sheet can be placed over this on which to draw in variations and other details. This enables you to build up and alter at will the plan until you are completely satisfied with it. Then it can be transferred to the graph paper to form a master plan.

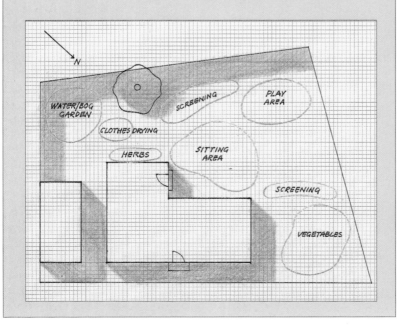

Steven Wooster/Garden Picture Library

Eric Crichton

A well-kept vegetable patch (above) can be happily integrated with flower beds in a small garden.

By creating a variety of separate areas, the owner has made the most of this garden (left). Shrubs and trees provide privacy and screen unsightly sheds. The curved borders and lawn make the rectangular area seem bigger. A seat has been included and the pond provides a feature of interest at the far end. The washing line runs alongside the path.

Buddleia (right) is a fast-growing shrub that soon provides a splash of colour.

Neil Holmes

sible to have them somewhere nearer to the house.

Vegetable gardens can be made to look very ornamental, especially if laid out in geometric beds with grass or gravel paths between – they certainly do not have to be an eyesore and hidden away.

Areas for sitting

Some sort of sitting and outdoor living area is important and most people opt for a patio. This should be sited in the sunniest part of the garden, ideally adjacent to the house.

Many people like a lawn as well, but in a small garden constant use can turn this into a threadbare mud patch.

An open area other than a patio (which, in any case, may be partially enclosed to shelter it from the wind) is strongly recommended. It gives a sense of space in a garden and avoids that 'shut-in' feeling. A small garden, especially, needs this. The alternative to a lawn is a gravel area, constructed from pea shingle over a firm bed of well-rammed soil.

Sun and shade

A garden should have both sunny and shady areas, to suit people and plants. On a brand new site, plan at the outset for some shady areas. Include a group of small trees or large shrubs, both of which should

Broom (left) is a shrub that can be planted for a quick effect. This is Genista hispanica, which is commonly known as Spanish gorse.

A small, square garden (below) can be made functional yet attractive, with a central paved area and a variety of plants in containers, borders and protruding beds. A table and bench provide somewhere for tea, and the eye is caught by the lamppost and its surrounding variegated shrub.

cast dappled shade.

A garden exposed to full sun for much of the day can be an uncomfortable and glaring place, and you will not be able to grow the huge range of shade-loving plants.

For a quick effect, plan for some groups of large, fast-growing shrubs, such as buddleias or different varieties of brooms and pyracanthas.

Other features

These are some of the basic elements of good garden design but you may well require other features. However, do not be too adventurous. Bear in mind that some garden features can be very labour intensive and involve you in considerable time and money spent on maintenance.

A rock garden is a case in point. You will need to spend a lot of time on it weeding, if you want it always to look good.

A practical alternative, and one perhaps more appropriate in the garden of a modern house, is to have a small gravel area in which to grow al-

pines or rock plants. The gravel looks good and prevents weeds from growing.

Choose a sunny, well-drained part of the garden for this. It can have a few specimen rocks set in it and will make a very attractive and labour-saving feature.

A pond is a very popular feature but avoid it at all costs if you have small children. Instead, start off with a sunken sandpit for the toddlers, then when they grow up a bit convert it to a pond by removing the sand and lining it with a plastic or rubber pond liner.

Remember, though, a pond needs a fair amount of attention to keep it looking good. And it must be sited in a sunny part of the garden away from the shade of overhanging trees and large shrubs.

Practical points

A clothes drying area is important for many people. In a small garden, especially, a collapsible rotary drier set on a patio or lawn is often the most convenient solution.

If you want a greenhouse and have a fairly large garden, then it makes sense to site it near the house if you are going to run electricity and water to it. Running these services a considerable distance down a garden can be very expensive.

Besides, a greenhouse gen-

A contrast between hard landscape and rich borders (right) can be very effective. Here, pale gravel, square paving stones, circular stepping stones and the white statue are set off by the dark background of cypresses and bright floral arrangements. The light, Mediterranean feel is enhanced by the brown amphora and a spiky succulent in a matching brown jar.

Henk Dijkman/Garden Picture Library

Pat Brindley

erally needs frequent attention, which it may not get if sited too far from the house.

Pergolas are extremely popular and are well worth having. They are attractive in their own right, especially when spanning a path, and make ideal supports for climbing plants. Pergolas can also be built against unsightly outbuildings, such as concrete garages, to help hide them.

Making changes

In a well-established garden you may have some or all of these features. It is up to you which of them you retain.

Never be afraid to get rid of any features that you do not

like or require. Some people are reluctant to dig up paths, lawns, shrubs or trees, but remember that all of these, and other features, can be replaced if need be.

For a garden to be successful, it has got to be what you want, not what the previous owners required.

However, good advice on taking over an established garden is to leave it alone for a complete year. This will give you ample time to decide which features you want to retain and what you would like to replace.

Also, it will allow you to assess the plants. You may, for instance, have some attractive

shrubs, whose beauty was not obvious when you moved in.

The garden may be rich in bulbs and herbaceous perennials; remember these have a period of dormancy and so may well be hidden under the soil when you take over the house.

Most very old, worn-out shrubs are not worth keeping, but some can be rejuvenated by cutting them back hard in late winter or early spring. Roses respond well to this, as do shrubs like rhododendrons, laurels and yews.

Do, however, try to retain as many large shrubs and other plants as you can, for these help to create a real sense of maturity in a garden.

How to *Implement Your Plans*

Once you have drawn up a design, the next stage is to implement your plans. Tackle the various features in order of priority, to spread the workload – and expense.

Harry Smith Collection

If you are altering an existing garden, it is easy to plan the job in stages. But if you are starting to design a garden from scratch, the temptation is to try and do everything at once. For most people, this is a mistake, as apart from getting bogged down in the work, they will probably run out of cash leaving lots of depressing, half-finished projects.

Phasing the work
The answer is to decide on your priorities, and start on the most important features first. Good initial projects include building patios and paths, laying lawns and creating boundaries (such as walls and hedges). These can be done at most times of year, though autumn or spring is preferable. The next stage is planting, starting with a year round framework of ever-

Whatever the size or shape of the garden, adding a new feature or two will give it a fresh look. Frame an existing patio with a border to separate it from the lawn (above), but be sure to take precise measurements before even starting to dig.

Photos Horticultural

greens and trees, followed by smaller, fast-growing shrubs, herbaceous plants and roses.

If you want special features such as a pond, pergola, greenhouse or a self-contained 'theme' garden, their construction is best left till later when the main garden has been well established.

Patio

Loose-laid slabs tend to tip after a time and allow weeds to grow in between them, so mortar them on to a base of hardcore. Create planting pockets, if you wish, by leaving out some slabs; remove hardcore from these areas and substitute topsoil.

To ensure the patio is a good

If a path (above) is required, put it at the top of the list of planned tasks. It is far easier to add flower beds or herbaceous borders after paths, boundaries and other 'fixed' features have been constructed.

Hardy and fast-growing, the bright blue flowers of Ceratostigma willmottianum (right) can add a splash of colour to a garden.

Walls are the most expensive type of boundary but they provide patios with the best form of shelter from the wind. Attractive pierced concrete blocks (below) give additional visual interest.

Photos Horticultural

bits are in the bottom layer.

However, 'minor' paths designed to allow you to amble gently round the garden enjoying the flowers need not be so solidly constructed. You can sink paving slabs straight into the soil or a lawn in stepping-stone fashion.

Lawn

The foundation of a lawn is the soil beneath it, so dig in as much organic matter as possible before sowing seed or turfing. Turf can be laid at any time from early autumn to late spring except when the ground is very wet or frozen; seed is always best sown in autumn or early spring.

Boundaries

Walls are the most permanent form of garden boundary but they are also the most expensive. Any wall over about 60cm/2ft high will need concrete foundations and a pillar approximately every 2m/6ft to help support it. Bed the base of fence posts in rubble and concrete; metal fence post supports can be used but they are much less firm.

As an alternative to a solid fence, make a light screen by nailing trellis to posts and use this as a base for growing

Peter McHoy

suntrap, create extra shelter round two or three sides with evergreen plants, walls or fences. Or build screens of trellis secured to strong uprights, and plant with climbers.

Paths

Paths that will be used regularly should be constructed of concrete, or paving slabs with proper foundations. Even gravel paths last longer if the gravel is laid over a base of well rolled hardcore, graduated in size so the largest

TREES FOR SMALL GARDENS

Acer pseudoplatanus 'Brilliantissimum', 3m/10ft, bronze-pink young foliage
Acer negundo 'Flamingo', 3m/10ft, variegated leaves, pink-tinged in spring.
Snowy mespilus (*Amelanchier lamarckii*) 3.6m/12ft, spring blossom and bronzy new foliage, followed by red berries and autumn tints.
Buddleia alternifolia 3.6m-4.5m/12-15ft, lilac flowered shrub, best trained as tree
Judas tree *(Cercis siliquastrum)* 4.5m/15ft, rounded leaves, pink flowers.
Gleditsia triacanthos 'Sunburst', 4.5m/15ft, bright gold, mimosa-like foliage
Laburnum 'Vossii' 4.5m/15ft, yellow flowers like bunches of grapes.
Crab apples *(Malus)* , 3.6-4.5m/12-15ft, 'John Downie' flask-shaped, rosy-orange fruit; 'Golden Hornet' round yellow fruit; 'Maypole' upright, single stemmed branchless tree.
Mulberry *(Morus nigra)*, 5-8m/15-20ft, prettily shaped tree with heart-shaped leaves, gnarled scaly bark, and fruit in summer.

Photos Horticultral

The deciduous Judas tree (left) provides profuse pink flowers from mid-spring onwards, followed by long, purplish-red pods in late summer. It should be planted in a sunny position in well-drained soil.

Here a scree bed (right) makes an informal but effective feature.

Constructing a light screen such as a trellis (below) secured to strong supports is an easy way to turn a patio into a suntrap. Add a few fast-growing climbers, hanging baskets and containers to make a very pleasant outdoor seating and eating area.

Beech hedging (below right) creates a good boundary but remember that it will take up more room than a wall or fence and is not fast-growing.

climbers – this looks particularly good round a patio.

Hedges are good natural boundaries, but take several years to establish. They also take up rather more room than a wall or fence.

Plant deciduous hedging from mid autumn to early spring, and evergreen in early autumn or mid spring for best results. Plant in a staggered row, and cut plants down hard so they start branching from the base. Repeat hard pruning annually for the first few years for a dense hedge.

Beds and borders
Work out the exact measurements from your plan (see Planning Your Garden 1, pages 902-907), and mark out with canes. Lay a hosepipe round the canes, and use this with considerable care as a guide for digging the bed.

Ron Sutherland/Garden Picture Library

Photos Horticultural

Strip the turf off first. This can be used elsewhere. Then dig deeply, adding organic matter and grit if it is clay soil. Sprinkle Growmore or blood, fish and bone, and rake in, levelling the soil surface as you go before planting.

Vegetables and fruit

Prepare soil as above. Container-grown fruit trees and bushes can be planted in summer, though it is better to do so in autumn or spring.

If there is a lack of space, plant a row of cordon-trained fruit trees and bushes to screen off the vegetable plot from the rest of the garden. Or plant a mixed ornamental fruit and vegetable bed.

Pond

Excavate the pond to the desired shape and size. Before adding a lining of butyl rubber or nylon-reinforced PVC, line the hole with old newspapers to prevent sharp stones perfor-

ating the liner and causing leaks. Do this construction work in autumn and fill the pond. Plant and stock it in spring. The addition of a fountain or waterfall and a biological filter will help keep the water clear.

Scree bed

Prepare the bed in autumn or winter. Mark out the site and build dwarf walls of bricks and mortar, stone walling blocks or dry natural stone. Place a layer of broken bricks, building rubble and so on, in the base for drainage. Infill with a 50:50 mixture of soil and grit or gravel. Plant in early spring, then spread a 2.5-5cm/1-2in layer of stone chippings between plants. This sets them off nicely and will help to prevent neck rot.

Trees

Check ultimate height and spread before planting a tree in small gardens. Only small

Andrew Lawson

GARDEN NOTES

TAMING AN OVERGROWN SITE

Kill persistent perennial weeds by watering with brushwood killer. Alternatively, cut back by hand or hire a rotary scythe, and treat re-growth with a glyphosate-based weedkiller (several treatments may be needed). You can also cut back, sow grass, and keep it mowed – perennial weeds cannot stand regular cutting.

Remove old or dangerous trees, especially those whose roots are endangering nearby drains or foundations. Where large trees are concerned, call in a professional tree surgeon. Have stumps winched out, or get in a stump grinder to remove them.

Smaller trees can be cut back to a stump, killed with brushwood killer, and then planted with climbers.

A SUNKEN SAND PIT

Dig a hole to the required size.

1 Cut a piece of 12mm/½in exterior grade plywood into four strips slightly smaller than the hole. Nail an offcut of 5-7.5cm/2-3in square timber at each corner.

2 Put the wooden framework in the hole, then backfill the sides with sand. Level the base and spread 5cm/2in gravel. Cover with a sheet of heavy-duty polythene perforated with small holes every 10cm/4in. Fill with washed silver sand.

3 Cut a piece of exterior-grade plywood for the lid to the size of the pit, then nail four 5 × 2.5cm/2 × 1in battens to the underside. Treat with preservative.

4 Or cut and join pieces of tongued-and-grooved timber. Nail three 5 × 2.5cm/ 2 × 1in battens to the underside. Treat with preservative.

Michael Shoebridge

Shrubs such as Hibiscus syriacus 'Blue Bird' (below) can always be relied on to quickly cover the very barest walls and fences.

to medium-sized ornamental trees with small root systems can be safely planted fairly close to houses. Avoid planting woodland or forest trees, which will become too large, and avoid siting trees or shrubs close to underground drains as their roots can penetrate and eventually block them. (Willows, poplars and hydrangeas are particularly bad trees and shrubs to plant near drains.)

Gardens in gardens

Self-contained areas such as a herb garden or formal flower garden are currently extremely fashionable. Keep the area separate from the rest of the garden by creating a screen (fence, wall or hedge) with an archway or gate leading in. First, lay hard surfaces such as paths then prepare soil, and plant in spring.

Use tubs, urns, trimmed box trees in pots, topiary-trained yew or hedging, forcing pots and so on for decoration. Edge beds with a mini-hedge of dwarf box or lavender in a formal garden, or use rows of tiles or bricks.

Children's play area

Where possible, provide a separate play area for children. Instead of grass which wears out quickly, surface it with bark chippings – they look good and are soft and resilient. Surround the area with thin logs or shuttering to retain chippings. Install swings, climbing frames, play houses and so on, and if there is an overhanging tree, you can also add an old car tyre dangling from a rope.

A sandpit can also be provided; this can either be dug into the ground or made as a small, raised bed filled with sand.

Garden buildings

Garden buildings are mostly bought in sections ready to erect. Check all parts are present and in good condition on delivery.

Read and understand the instructions before starting to assemble. Prepare any foundations or construct bases first, and allow concrete to dry.

Choose a fine day for building, arrange helpers for heavy lifting jobs, and always have everything neatly laid out ready to start.

Derek Gould

Landscaping Small Gardens

By applying a few simple principles used by landscape gardeners, you can turn a dull plot into something really special, full of interesting shapes and surprises.

Ron Sutherland/Garden Picture Library

Steven Wooster/Garden Picture Library

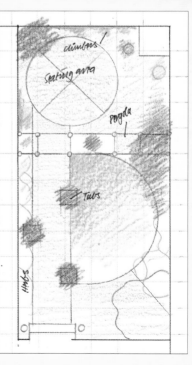

The first step in redesigning your garden is to make a scale plan of the site (below left), on which you can plot where the various elements – lawn, paths, beds, shed, paved seating area and so on – will go. Then, unless you envisage only small-scale changes or are skilled at D.I.Y., it is time to seek professional help in turning your plans into reality.

This may well mean you have to put up for a while with your garden resembling a cross between a building site and a war zone (above left) as the basic structure – the paths, paving and any wooden structures – is put in place. It is only when the plants come to be put in and the lawn laid that the site comes to resemble a garden, ready for you to add personal touches such as ornaments and garden furniture (far left).

Once a garden has been designed as well as this, maintaining it is simply a matter of looking after the plants and applying the odd coat of paint.

Few of us can afford the services of a professional landscape gardener. However, by applying the basic principles they use, and maybe putting in a bit of hard work at the start, you can make your garden infinitely more interesting, whatever its size. A typical town garden with a rectangle of grass surrounded by straight flowerbeds and raw-looking fences can be improved out of all recognition by redesigning its basic shape.

If you are starting a new garden, either from a bare patch left by the builders, or from an overgrown or neglected old plot, thinking on landscape gardening lines right from the start will stop you making mistakes that take time and money to put right later on. A well-designed garden will be easier to manage and can be perfectly attuned to your specific needs.

Design principles

The ground rules that professional landscape gardeners follow are basically simple, and can be learnt by studying other gardens, either on the ground or in photographs. A visually pleasing garden always has plenty of curves – lawns and beds have gently undulating edges, and paths wind away into the distance.

Strategically placed focal points – a sundial, bird bath, large flower tub or specimen tree – draw your eye onwards and provide extra interest. If there is an interesting feature or pleasant view beyond the garden, this will be framed in foliage to accentuate it.

The garden will probably be designed so that you **cannot** quite see how far it extends, or exactly what happens when

---

CHOOSING A STYLE

The most popular style of garden is the natural-looking, informal one – but there are plenty of others you can choose.

Formal A symmetrical design featuring angular shapes and formal structures like pergolas and vistas with straight paths, framed in arches, leading to a distant focal point.

Cottage Flower garden packed with traditional native flowers reached from almost invisible winding paths; roses and clematis on every wall. Should not really have a lawn.

Architectural Small garden with built features in bold shapes – paving, brick planters, formal pool. Minimal planting with bold-leafed plants.

Japanese Small-scale landscape of raked gravel, boulders, water with bridge, Japanese stoneware, shrubs, bonsai; no grass.

Woodland/wild Deciduous trees underplanted with rhododendrons, ferns or woodland flowers. Natural paths (stone or packed earth).

Long grass, natural-shaped pond with bog garden attached, native hedging, wild flowers.

Paved/courtyard Mediterranean feel, semi-formal, attractively paved. Classical pots, urns, statuary; raised formal pool or wall fountain. Main planting in containers and against walls.

Even a small yard garden can be landscaped (left); the same principles apply. Where a lawn was the feature of the similarly-shaped, slightly larger garden on the opposite page, here wooden decking has been used to provide slight changes of height, a pathway through the garden and a seating area. As the site is rather dark, foliage plants in containers and borders provide growing interest, while the narrowness of the garden has been made an advantage by laying wooden beams from wall to wall to create an arbour.

Ron Sutherland/Garden Picture Library

Andrew Lawson

Ron Sutherland/Garden Picture Library

Dividing a garden up into small areas is a necessity for a long narrow plot. A wooden trellis (above) is perfect for this. It both screens and reveals, and acts as a windbreak and a support for climbers.

As an alternative, a smaller area can be divided up with paths; paving (below) creates strong geometric shapes, while other materials such as grass or gravel can make curved or serpentine edges.

you get to the end – it invites you to explore. This can be done quite simply by partially blocking the view with a trellis and an arch, or inserting a bed running crossways that is planted with tallish shrubs.

However lavishly planted, even wild, the garden may seem at first, it will always consist of clearly defined areas. Lawns, flowerbeds, paths and a paved sitting area are the most common features, but there may also be a vegetable garden, children's play area, a

pond – as many different areas of interest as the size of the plot can comfortably take.

Changes of level are also built into the design – terraces, steps and grassy banks in a large garden, raised beds or a rockery in a smaller one. Even if the garden is actually flat, the planting will provide eye interest at different levels – ground cover, herbaceous plants, taller shrubs, climbing plants and trees.

Changes of texture are equally important – a close-

clipped lawn sets off a luxuriant herbaceous border; hard paving contrasts with soft delicate flowers; smooth, still water reflects rugged stone.

Providing privacy is an important part of the landscape gardener's brief. Boundaries will be designed to provide this unobtrusively, without creating a prison-yard feeling.

The first step in redesigning your garden is to decide to what use you are going to put

Ron Sutherland/Garden Picture Library

A well-planned garden has something for everyone. A sandpit (above) encourages young children to use the garden and provides the garden with a focal point. It can be converted into a formal pond later.

Remarkable effects can be obtained by reversing the usual order of things (below). Here a raised central lawn is encircled by a water feature, with more conventional beds filling in around the edges.

it. Is it to be an outdoor room, used mainly for relaxation? Or do you have time to care for lots of flowers and a lawn? Will it need to cater for children playing? What about special features like a pond, rockery, sunken garden, barbecue, or easy-to-maintain raised beds?

Shapes and sizes

The next step is to measure your plot on all sides, to see if it is actually rectangular, or whether it tapers or is irregularly shaped. Make a note of any slopes, and find out which parts of the garden are in sun or shade at which times of day. List features you wish to keep, like established trees or shrubs, and those you want to get rid of, like piles of rubble or dilapidated sheds.

Draw a scale plan of the garden on squared paper. Include the position of the house and anything you are quite certain is going to stay, like a large tree or paved area.

Get several photocopies made, and use one to draw a plan of the garden as it is. Use the others to see how you can create the garden of your dreams. Rough out the broad concept first – in pencil to allow for changes of mind – leaving details of planting and so

on until later.

Do not try to cram too many features into a small garden. Drawing your ideas to scale on paper will make you realize what you can and cannot get into your particular plot.

Paths need to be at least 60cm/2ft wide for easy movement. However, paths are not essential; unless the ground is very boggy, close-mown grass can take their place.

A large lawn that fills most of the width makes a small garden look bigger – like fitted carpet in a small room. The depth of the flower beds should ideally be in proportion to the size of the plot.

Long and narrow

Make the most of a typical long narrow plot by including features that run across the garden – beds with tall planting, internal hedges or trellis work – at intervals on alternate sides. Another way of creating the illusion of width is to set the lawn at an angle of 45° to the house.

A small, square garden looks best with interest in the centre – a round lawn or a central pool or tree. Take away the squareness with curved beds in the corners. An irregular shape lends itself to the

LABOUR-SAVERS

● Have mowing stones round the lawn to reduce the edging chore. Do not have island beds.
● In a small or front garden, get rid of the grass and have a gravel garden instead.
● A pond, once installed, is labour-saving as there is almost no weeding.
● For almost zero maintenance, pave the garden and plant dwarf conifers, heathers, no-prune shrubs and bulbs.
● Cut down weeding by planting plenty of smothering ground-cover plants.

GARDEN NOTES

Ugly but functional buildings need covering up (above). This unsightly garage has all but vanished under a Boston ivy (Parthenocissus tricuspidata).

By introducing steps into your garden, you create changes of height and divide up the garden (below). They are also a handy place to put container plants.

BRIGHT IDEAS

DISGUISES

Some unsightly features can be disguised or totally transformed by planting.

● Dead tree. Grow honeysuckle or a clematis up it and put a circular seat round the base, or cut the top level and turn it into a bird table.

● Cracked concrete. Plant creeping plants like thyme in the crevices. Enlarge broken areas, fill with compost and plant alpines.

● Ugly outbuilding. Clad concrete walls with weatherboard. Fix horizontal wires to timber and plant an evergreen honeysuckle. Russian vine or *Clematis montana* will soon cover both walls and roof.

● Straight concrete path. Soften edges with tumbling, low-growing plants.

creation of several distinct 'mini-gardens', divided by internal hedges or screens.

Some gardens taper off very unsatisfactorily into a triangle at the bottom. Depending on its size, you can cut this off with a big, ground-hugging evergreen shrub, or screen it off with trellis and climbing plants. Create a secret garden in the enclosure – or use it as an area in which to tuck away the shed or compost heap.

Treat a minute garden or walled yard like an outdoor room, with attractive paving, lots of pretty plant containers, raised beds and garden ornaments. Train climbers up the walls for vertical interest. High walls often mean deep shade – paint them white to a height of 1.8m/6ft (so frequent repainting is easy) for maximum light reflection, and choose light-coloured paving. A sunny walled yard, warm and sheltered, is an ideal site for a scented garden.

Once you have roughed things out on paper, get outside and see how it will look in three dimensions. Use bamboo

Photos Horticultural

canes to mark the position of any tall features or partitions; pegs and string to map out possible new paths; and a hosepipe or rope to experiment with curves in a flower bed or lawn.

Making it work

Check that the features you planned on paper will work. Herbaceous borders need a sunny spot to flower really well. A pond should get a reasonable amount of sun and be

away from trees. Although a patio is usually sited close to the house, if it is on the shady side of the building think about putting it elsewhere.

A lawn needs sun for at least part of the day to flourish – but you can buy special seed mixes for shade. Use the least sunny parts of your garden for shade-loving shrubs, ground cover plants, and utilitarian items like sheds and compost bins, screened if necessary.

Slight slopes are manageable, but on sharp ones soil gets washed to the bottom, and grass is difficult to mow. Some form of terracing is the answer to this problem.

Sometimes the problem can be solved by dividing the slope into two or more terraces by inserting shallow log steps, and confining the soil with peat blocks, old railway sleepers or low drystone walls. On sharper slopes the downward pressure is much greater and solidly built masonry walls and steps will be needed – this is almost certainly a job for a professional.

Another way of dealing with

Paths that wind off out of sight always add to the sense of space in a garden, and give it an air of intrigue and mystery (above left), though this is not always easy to appreciate when seen from above. It is always a good idea to try and visualize how a new garden scheme will look from the ground as well as from the house.

Although bricks and paving are the usually favoured material for making steps and paths, there are other possibilities (above right). Railway sleepers are strong and weather resistant and will take a dark wood preservative, enabling you to make a flight of steps with contrasting gravel 'treads' and wooden 'risers'.

a slope is to turn it into a rock garden by building rocks into it. However, this is heavy work and may prove expensive; stone is costly, and what looks like a lot does not go very far once half-buried in the ground.

Getting help

Nasties like crumbling concrete or tarmac hardstanding, disused sheds and ancient rubbish tips cannot be designed round or lived with – they must be swept away. Hire a skip if you can manage the clearance yourself, or look in the Yellow Pages under garden services and get some idea of cost.

Garden labourers are also invaluable if you have a totally overgrown plot needing rotovating, an old hedge or dead tree trunk to be grubbed out, earth to be moved or a pond dug. Alternatively you can hire rotovators, hedge-cutters, heavy-duty mowers and flame guns by the day or weekend.

If you have a big tree that needs thinning, look in the Yellow Pages under tree work – never tackle it yourself.

A Lawn From Seeds

Sowing your own lawn is both cheap and easy, and gives excellent results. The key to success lies in preparing the ground thoroughly first and time spent in initial preparation will be reflected in the end result.

New lawns can be created from seed or by laying turf. There are pros and cons to each method, but there is no doubt that seeding is cheaper.

A lawn is usually one of the major features of a garden, and perhaps the one we take most for granted. Most of us hope to get away with weekly cutting and edging, and occasionally dealing with broad-leaved weeds. To make this possible, the secret is proper preparation of the ground. Time spent on initial preparation will pay off later.

Shape and position

The first things to consider when creating a lawn are its shape, size, level and position.

Rectangular lawns with sharp corners and straight edges look right in a formal context but are harder to maintain well. A curving outline will allow you to mow with much less stopping and turning. This means cutting will be faster and you are less likely, especially when the ground is wet, to damage the lawn when turning the mower.

Lawns look better without too many beds or trees. It may be worth extending a bed to include a tree, in order to leave a long clean edge to the lawn.

Choosing the area

There is no point in trying to put down to lawn land which is unsuitable for grass. For instance, grass will never grow well in deep shade under trees, even when using one of the grass seed mixtures in-

tended for shade. And boggy, ill-drained parts of the garden will always be a problem as lawn, unless you undertake some serious land drainage first. Try to site your lawn in the open, on soil which is naturally adequately drained.

Having decided on the extent of your lawn-to-be, you can begin to prepare the ground. Ideally this should be done in the autumn, ready for spring sowing, but it can be prepared in the summer for sowing in late summer or early autumn. The procedure for autumn sowing is exactly the same but instead of leaving the ground roughly dug for the

Existing paths and beds of shrubs (above) in an established garden may dictate the shape of your lawn. For ease of maintenance keep the number of beds within a lawn to a minimum. In the garden of a new house you will have more flexibility.

Photos Horticultural

SEED MIXTURES

Seed mixtures are designed to produce different types of lawn. They contain different species of grass according to how short they are to be cut, how hard-wearing they are, and how much light they need. The tougher mixtures usually contain ryegrass, which gives them strength but also a coarse texture. For a finer lawn, not intended for heavy use, choose a mixture without ryegrass.

You will usually find a slightly higher application rate recommended for the finer mixtures, as they are slower to establish and more

The way your lawn is to be used will determine your choice of a suitable seed mixture.

likely to suffer from the competition of weeds in the early stages.

Marshall Cavendish

Peter McHoy

frost to break down over the winter, you must cultivate it manually there and then.

If the land you wish to make lawn is already under grass, or has perennial, deep-rooted weeds in it, like dandelion and dock, it is best to use a weed-killer on the ground in the autumn. Use, for example, a herbicide such as Tumbleweed that contains glyphosate.

Many lawns begin life from the bare soil of a building site around new houses. This often means that there are chunks of rubble to be removed before work can begin. It also means, all too often, that subsoil from the house's foundation will

On the left (above) a ryegrass mix with some coarser grasses, contrasted with, right, a fine grass mix.

A town garden (below) with a semi-circle of grass that has a wavy edge to accommodate flower beds and tubs.

have been spread over the top-soil. This needs to be dug off, especially if it is clay subsoil, to get back to the proper top-soil. This will restore the natural drainage and means your lawn will be rooting into fertile topsoil instead of leaner subsoil. Do not be tempted to dig the subsoil into the topsoil and hope for the best. It will only lead to problems later.

Digging

Having got back to the topsoil and killed the existing vegetation, the ground can be rough dug, just as you would a vegetable patch, and left in large clods for the winter frosts to break down. If the land has had heavy machinery on it, then it is worth digging to two spade-depths. Otherwise one good spade-depth is sufficient.

On poor, thin soils this is also the time to incorporate any compost or well-rotted manure you have available, to increase the soil's fertility and

Ron Sutherland/Garden Picture Library

GROWING TIPS

RESEEDING

If any bare patches appear after germination, lightly reseed them using the same mixture. Remember to save some seed for the purpose, rather than sowing it all at the outset.

IMPROVING SOIL

During the winter, test the soil's pH, to see how acidic or alkaline it is. Do not over-lime, but if the soil is very acidic, then 85g/3oz of ground limestone to the square metre/yard will probably put matters right.

Heavy clay soils will benefit from the addition of 4.5kg/10lb of coarse, gritty sand to each square metre, incorporated into the soil, like the lime, with the spring digging.

Marshall Cavendish

Peter McHoy

moisture retentiveness.

In late winter or early spring the rough-dug land should be dug over again, breaking down the lumps to leave a smoother surface. Work in well any grit, lime or compost that has been added. A rotovator is excellent for this purpose if you have the muscles to handle one, or can make

Peter McHoy

use of someone else's muscles! Afterwards the surface can be raked roughly level and any stones picked off.

Between now and the time to sow the grass seed, unsuitable grasses and weed seedlings, such as chickweed and shepherd's purse, will spring up in mild spells. The more that germinate now the better.

Once the soil has been dug over, tread it (above) to firm the ground. Work up and down, breaking up any clods. Rake it and then tread it again in the other direction. Seed can be broadcast by hand (below left). Working from a string line will ensure even coverage.

You can easily hoe off the seedlings or spray them with a contact weedkiller such as weedol, based on paraquat with diquat. The more weeds you can eliminate, the better the seedling grasses will grow.

A week or two before you are ready to sow, scatter a handful of Growmore or a similar balanced fertilizer over each

Eric Crichton

square metre/yard and rake it in thoroughly. This will give the seedling grasses a little boost to get them going.

Firming the surface

Now the ground has been dug and broken down, it needs to be consolidated to give an even, level surface.

On a dry day, tread the soil down firmly all over with your heels, working in lines up and down the soil. Then rake it over to fill any depressions that have appeared. Repeat the process in the opposite direction and rake again. Work the soil surface with the rake, removing small stones and bits of root, until you have a smooth, fine surface, with no bumps, hollows or soft spots. You can now sow the seed.

Seed sowing

Most garden centres stock well-known, reliable brands of grass seed, supplied in various mixtures of species, which will

GARDEN NOTES

WEEDING AND FEEDING

Until the new turf is established, weed seedlings should be removed by hand when they are large enough to handle. Selective weed killers should not be used for the first six months as they can harm the young grasses.

A new lawn on well-prepared soil will require no further feeding for several months at least. Autumn-sown lawns should not be fed until the following spring, as late feeding can lead to fungal diseases attacking the young growth.

give you the turf suitable for different kinds of lawn. Before you buy, decide whether you want a very fine, ornamental lawn which will not be hard-wearing, or something tougher

Photos Horticultural

Grass seedlings coming through (above) on a newly sown lawn. Unfortunately the surface has been poorly prepared, leaving too many clods and stones which will prevent seedlings growing. The clods will be broken up when the lawn is rolled but the stones will have to be raked off to prevent damage to the mower blades.

A pot standing in the middle of a lawn (left) can be as effective as a flower bed. It can be moved when it comes to mowing.

for children to play on, or perhaps something to tolerate shade. Check the recommendations for use on the packet, and also check the advised rate of application.

A rough rule of thumb for seeding lawns is 30-45/1-1½oz per square metre/yard. Increasing the rate does not necessarily lead to a better, faster lawn, as densely sown seedlings can easily damp off and die. Stick to the manufacture's recommendations, and select seed treated with fungicide and bird-repellant.

Choose a dry day to sow the

MOWING

When the seedling grasses are 2.5cm/1in high they can be rolled to firm them in. At about 4cm/1½in the grass can have its first cut with a mower, down to about 2.5cm/1in. Continue to top off the grass at that height until it becomes established. Then you can begin to lower the blades to 1.5cm/½in. Autumn-sown lawns will probably only need two or three cuts before winter. Take care not to let autumn leaves lie on the new grass or it will die out beneath them.

seed, when the soil surface is dry but there is plenty of moisture underneath. First rake the soil surface lightly, then scatter the seed over the soil, covering the whole lawn twice, first in one direction, then in the other, using half the mixture in each direction. This should help to rule out any bare patches. Alternatively, you can borrow seed spreaders from some garden centres when you buy the seed. These can be useful for larger lawns.

Final touches

Now rake again very lightly, just to turn in the seed and cover it. Inevitably some seed will remain on the surface, but sowing rates allow for losses to wind and birds.

There is no need to roll or water-in the seed. Simply let it germinate. Sprinklers can do harm by puddling the surface, so only water if the soil really begins to dry out. If the ground is very dry, water two or three days before you sow. Germination times vary according to temperature and humidity levels, but the finer grasses are generally the slowest. Patience is almost always rewarded!

SEED VERSUS TURF

There are advantages and disadvantages to the use of seed instead of turf when making a lawn.

	SEED	TURF
ADVANTAGES	Seed is cheaper. It is easier to put down. A greater choice of seed mixture and type of grass is available. Sowing can be delayed.	The lawn is usable much sooner, in eight to ten weeks.
DISADVANTAGES	The ground needs finer preparation. The lawn is slower to become usable: autumn-sown lawns will be ready next summer, spring-sown lawns will be ready that autumn.	Cheaper meadow turf contains weeds and poorer grasses, and costs much more than sowing seed. Fine turf, grown from seed, is even more expensive, but very good. Turf is hard work to lay. Turf must be laid without delay once it has been delivered.

A lawn sown with 'Hunter' grass seed mixture in mid-autumn has made good progress by late winter (right). By early summer, when it will have been rolled and then mown several times, it will be ready for use.

A circular lawn (below) is easy to mow in ever decreasing circles. If a small lawn like this, surrounded by a brick wall, were square it would be much more difficult to mow.

A well-nourished, carefully tended lawn (facing page) is an integral part of a traditional English garden. It is used to unify the often diverse features of a garden and provides the perfect foil for the trees and flowering shrubs.

A Touch of Formality

Introduce a touch of formality into your plot, no matter what its size. Whether you choose simply to add a statue or to transform your whole garden, here are some great ideas to get you started.

Andrew Lawson

If you wish to create a garden that is well ordered and neat, with straight paths and formal flower beds, a tidy patio and a well-trimmed lawn – perhaps with a statue, bird bath or other decoration – then the classic ornamental garden is the right kind for you.

Whether planning your garden from scratch or making changes to your existing plot, do not make the mistake of considering the garden in isolation. Your design should also take into account the architecture of your home. An intricate design would look out of place next to a simple, modern house, for example.

Perfect symmetry

The overall effect you are looking for in an ornamental garden is one of clean, simple, uncluttered lines. Beds, borders, patios, lawns and other features need to be geometric in shape. They also need to form part of an overall symmetry.

In your quest for a harmonious design, no element should be left 'out on a limb'. Your geometric-shaped flower-beds, for example, should be incorporated into the patio or lawn, or surrounded by neat paths.

Formal beds need formal planting. In spring, a carpet of forget-me-nots, polyanthus or wallflowers punctuated regularly with bedding tulips could be used. The bed could be

An ornamental garden need not be complicated in its design: this garden (left) is all the more pleasing for its simplicity. A pair of lemon trees in pots flank the doorway and a single terracotta urn provides an eye-catching central feature.

If you feel that a statue would be too grand for your garden, why not have a bird bath instead? This one (left) has been placed in the middle of a circular lawn. The round shapes of lawn and bowl are further echoed by the brick-edged bed at the base of the pedestal. As well as being a decorative feature in its own right, a bird bath will also attract birds to your garden.

small number of plants and colours. Go for single colours instead of mixtures when choosing bedding plants and aim to harmonize the beds with the colour of the house, paths, walls and fences.

Low levels

A classic ornamental feature worth considering is a sunken garden. These are usually square or rectangular and the depth should be in proportion

GROWING TIPS

A BEAUTIFUL LAWN

An untidy lawn can ruin the effect of an ornamental garden. If yours is a mess, do not despair. Rather than dig it up and start again, there are ways you can improve it.
● mow regularly and frequently to discourage the growth of coarse rye grasses and encourage finer grasses
● as well as regular cutting, feed frequently with a proprietary fertilizer
● to discourage moss, aerate the lawn in dry conditions and, if soil is acid, add lime
● after aerating, add a top dressing of sharp sand and rake it in
● children and dogs can damage the lawn, so if you really want it to look beautiful, don't allow them to play on the grass or it might end up looking like a football pitch!

edged broadly with a border of double daisies. If you have a group of formal beds, you could stick to the same scheme in each one or different, complementary plantings.

For summer, there are so many bedding plants from which to make your selection that there is an almost infinite variety of combinations.

The right plants

Effective schemes include a carpet of wax begonias or zonal pelargoniums punctuated with silver-leaved *Senecio bicolor*, with a centrepiece of tall cabbage palm (*Cordyline australis*). Remember, however, that these plants are not hardy enough to grow reliably out of doors unless you live in a mild or sheltered area.

Choose plants to suit your own particular climate and soil conditions, following a few simple style guidelines. For an uncluttered effect stick to a

PERFECT PARTNERS

It is best to keep to simple colour schemes in your ornamental garden – a mixture of hues could detract from the orderliness of the design. Here, the white tulip 'Pax' has been combined with 'Crystal Bowl' pansies.

When it comes to deciding on plants to fill your ornamental garden, the choice is huge – but there are some that seem especially 'right' for this style of design. Plants to go for are those that are tidy and echo the orderliness of your design.

Taller plants with straight, upright stems such as tulips can look very effective placed in a sea of neat, low-growing flowers such as pansies. The impressive crown imperial (*Fritillaria imperialis*) can be used in a similar way. When combining different plants, check that their flowering times are the same.

For a traditional touch, why not try a pair of standard roses, placed symmetrically in your design? Surround them with one of the more compact forms of lavender, such as Dutch lavender (*Lavandula vera*).

Many herbs are ideal plants for the ornamental garden, forming neat clumps and having the added appeal of aromatic foliage and a practical use in the kitchen, too. Combine blue-grey sage, golden balm and parsley.

AN 'ANTIQUE' CONTAINER

A new concrete container can look too bright and clean but by the clever application of a little paint you can easily 'age' it to blend in with its surroundings. Getting the exact shade you want is a matter of trial and error: what you are aiming for is a natural-looking stone colour. Do a test on a piece of scrap paper first.

This method can also be used for 'antiquing' plastic containers – but omit the last stage as sanding is likely to make the paint flake off.

You will need:
raw umber acrylic paint
black acrylic paint
white emulsion paint
2 paintbrushes
medium glass paper

1 *Assemble your materials before you begin. You can paint more than one container at a time.*

2 *Pour some emulsion into a jar and add small amount of raw umber acrylic paint. Paint the container.*

3 *Add more raw umber and dab on paint allowing the lighter base colour to show through.*

4 *Add some black paint to your mixture and paint the hollow parts, softening edges with a dry brush.*

5 *When the paint is dry, rub over the paint surface with glass paper to give a 'distressed' finish.*

Marshall Cavendish

BALANCING ACT

Two of the key things to watch out for when planning your ornamental garden are *symmetry* and *balance* – which simply means you should aim to get an equal balance between the different parts on opposite sides of the garden, borders or paths. A tall plant on one side should be matched by a similar plant, or ornament, on the other; a wide border could be balanced by a wide path. Neat, geometric shapes are also the right ones for your beds, paths and ponds.

to the area: the smaller the garden, the shallower it should be. Do not scale down your sunken garden too much, however. It should form a major part of the overall design of your ornamental garden. One possibility is to let it span the width of a narrow plot, creating a split-level effect. Changes of level will add an exciting new dimension to the look of your garden. As a guide, the depth should be about 30-60cm/12-24in.

Decorative details

The low retaining walls of your sunken garden can be built up with bricks. Ideally these should match the house, or be made from decorative concrete walling blocks.

For a really splendid effect, add a central feature such as a statue, sundial, most impressive of all, a small formal pool with a fountain.

Generally this is a wedge shape, broader at the base than at the top, with a rounded or flat top – but you can choose whichever shape you please, of course.

Hedges can also be used within the garden, to divide it into a number of areas. Separate the formal from the informal part of the garden if you have enough space.

Formal hedges should be 1.8m/6ft max. in height and will need regular clipping in the growing season to keep them in shape and prevent them from growing too tall.

Classic features

Low box hedges are an element in another classic formal garden feature, the *parterre*. This consists of geometric beds arranged in a regular pattern and set in a gravel area with space to walk between. The beds are edged with low hedges of dwarf box (*Buxus sempervirens* 'Suffruticosa'), which must be clipped regularly for a neat finish. The beds can be filled with seasonal

bedding or, if you want a more subtle, all-green look, with low-growing culinary and ornamental herbs.

Choosing accessories to dress up your formal garden is probably the most enjoyable part. Make your selection from the array of statues, sundials and ornamental containers you will find on display at most large garden centres.

Finishing touches

Use ornaments in moderation, as it is all too easy to go too far and ruin the simple, elegant effect you are aiming for. If space is limited, a well-chosen piece situated in the corner of the patio, beside a pool or at the far end of the lawn will be more effective than lots of little objects scattered all over the garden.

A statue is a good choice as a focal point, to draw the eye to a particular part of the garden. If you decide to put a statue in your garden, choose one that matches the scale of your plot. Avoid using a life-sized human figure if you have a pocket-

Your sunken garden can be laid out with geometric beds set in gravel or paving and planted with seasonal bedding, or you could create a formal rose garden.

A sunken rose garden can consist of a single bed or a group of geometric beds, perhaps set in a gravel or paved area or in a lawn. Choose formal roses such as large-flowered (hybrid tea) or cluster-flowered (floribunda) varieties. For tiny gardens, scale things down by using miniature roses.

Plant one variety per bed, perhaps with a standard rose, ideally of the same variety, in the centre of each bed, to give additional height.

Hedging bets

The boundaries of a formal ornamental garden are usually planted with formal hedges trained to a regular shape.

Statuary is very much part of the ornamental garden style. A well-placed statue can provide a bold focal point, leading the eye to a particular corner, and can form an essential part of the design. The circular area of gravel (above) cries out for some form of ornament to mark its centre: without the little trumpeter in the middle, it would have seemed very bare. The small figure holds the design together.

In another garden (right), cleverly placed urns and round paving slabs lead the eye naturally across the gravelled area to the statue on the far side. The dark, evergreen hedge behind it provides the perfect foil, accentuating the figure's form.

handkerchief-sized garden; a bust might be better, perhaps set on a pedestal or on a wall of a raised bed. Human figures and busts are suited to virtually any garden; those that are naked or carrying a vessel are probably most appropriate near water. If you have a pond, you may also like to consider placing a stone frog, fish or heron by the side of it.

If your statue is light in colour, set it against a dark background such as a hedge or brick wall. Set it next to a formal shrub such as a bay or fatsia, or soften its outlines with a climbing plant.

Modern wood

For an ultra-modern garden, you may prefer to choose a geometric object: a stone obelisk, pyramid, cube or sphere. Use a pair to flank a path or gateway, or place a single object so that it adds drama to a plain lawn or paved area.

A sundial mounted on a pedestal makes a good centrepiece for a sunken bed or the

In the restrained elegance of the ornamental garden, one of the pleasures you can enjoy is variety in colour and texture – and there are plenty of combinations to choose from. Here (left) the deep red of Begonia semperflorens contrasts with the yellow of Helichrysum petiolare 'Aureum' or 'Limelight'.

centre of a lawn. A container such as a stone urn can perform a similar function, while containers which are set in groups – ideally of similar design but not of the same size – can look extremely elegant.

Containers come in all shapes and sizes. A square wooden Versailles tub looks good in most settings and can be painted to match your

Harry Smith Collection

Andrew Lawson

GROWING TIPS

FORMAL HEDGES

These evergreen trees and shrubs are ideal for creating a boundary:

- box (*Buxus sempervirens*) is moderately slow-growing and needs frequent clipping, but forms a good, dense hedge
- Lawson cypress (*Chamaecyparis lawsoniana*) 'Green Hedger' is fast-growing and needs only annual clipping
- holly (*Ilex aquifolium*) is slow-growing, but dense if clipped regularly
- yew (*Taxus baccata*) is moderately slow-growing, but becomes very dense with regular clipping
- western red cedar (*Thuja plicata* 'Atrovirens') is a fast grower with fruity aromatic foliage and needs only annual trimming

---

cotta which creates a 'warm', rather rustic effect, and may be better suited to more informal parts of the garden. The most stylish -- and expensive – garden ornaments are made of stone, but reconstituted stone makes a good substitute. A decorative stone urn can be left unplanted and placed on a matching pedestal to grace a paved area or the centre of a rose garden.

Formal containers are best planted with neat, formal-looking plants – a mass of flowers and greenery tumbling

---

house. Rounded urns, vases and jars make good focal points, say at the end of a lawn, or as centrepieces for formal rose or sunken gardens. Containers also come in various different materials. At the cheaper end of the range, there is concrete and plastic. These materials may be cheap but in the long run they may be a false economy. Remember

The still surface of this rectangular pond (above left) is uncluttered by plants and calmly reflects the sky. This well-coordinated scheme (above right) has yellow Tagetes 'Lemon Gem' around the edge, with white begonias 'Silver Devil' and a single Artemisia 'Powis Castle' in the middle.

that your garden ornaments may be with you for years, and you may later regret not having splashed out a little more in the beginning to get something that is better quality and continues to be attractive.

Stylish stone

Next in the price range is glass-reinforced cement, a very presentable material, and terra-

loosely over the sides could spoil the tidy effect you have been working to achieve. Good choices would be clipped bay trees or perhaps some topiary in box or yew. You could even try a citrus tree, although if you live in one of the colder areas of the country you would need to bring this indoors into a greenhouse or a conservatory for the winter.

Creating Knot Gardens

With their roots deep in history, stylish knot gardens bring a sense of order and continuity to the garden, as well as a formal charm of their own.

Knot gardens originated in Italy, but were quickly adopted by Renaissance Europe. In England, they reached the height of their popularity in the 16th century. The notion of filling a square or rectangular plot with an intricate design, or knot, of low hedges, separating small areas of planting, appealed to Elizabethan gardeners, with their love of the formal.

Living history

Lately, knot gardens have been making a comeback. A modern knot garden brings an echo of a seemingly more gracious age and, with it, a sense of order and continuity.

Recent years have also seen a revival of interest in old fashioned or 'historical' plants. Nurseries specializing in old, even ancient, varieties of plants, including pansies, tulips, carnations, pinks and herbs, are flourishing. A knot garden can be a perfect setting for lovely old garden varieties.

The symmetrical, geometric shapes of knot gardens are adaptable and look equally good on a small or a grand scale. Obviously, the smaller the plot you have, the simpler the design should be.

Choosing a site

There are several things to bear in mind when choosing your site. Your design must start with a perfect square or rectangle, so the site must lend itself to that.

If you plan to fill you knots with plants, then the site must be in good sun. If the only area you have is shaded, all is not lost. You can use coloured gra-

vel instead of plants to enhance your design. This method has the added bonus of being easy to maintain. All that is needed is for the gravel to be raked and weeded and

the hedges trimmed to keep them neat.

Ideally, the site should be close to the house. Knot gardens are best appreciated from an upper storey, with the

The informal knot garden (above) is set off by a brick surround, while the more formal garden (facing page) maximises the potential of an open space.

Jerry Pavia/Garden Picture Library

36

Eric Crichton

Eric Crichton

GRAVEL OPTIONS

GARDEN NOTES

Coloured gravel is easy to find nowadays. Use two or, at the most, three colours that will complement each other.

For an authentic Elizabethan feel, use coarse chalk, coal and crushed or broken tiles or bricks instead of gravel. Sand makes a pleasing yellow colour. Chalk and coal mixed together make a grey-blue shade.

design laid out below you, like a living carpet.

Whether you are planning to fill a knot with plants or gravel, it is important to site it well away from overhanging trees. Soggy, dead leaves will clog up a knot and ruin the elegance of your design. Dead leaves will also discolour gravel, leaving it looking grubby instead of crisp and clean.

Tying a knot

Measure the site carefully, and draw a scaled down outline on graph paper. Experiment with fitting various shapes into your square or rectangle. Simple shapes make the best and most easily worked designs.

If you doubt your artistic skills, or you need some inspiration, your library should have books on garden design to help

DOUBLE THREADS

BRIGHT IDEAS

One lovely idea that was used in Elizabethan times was to make a double edging using contrasting hedging plants. Box and lavender make good companions, although rosemary, thyme or germander may be used too.

Another variation is to plant the two hedges with a gap between and to fill the gap with colourful flowers such as pansies.

This newly planted knot garden (above) has been raised above the level of the surrounding garden. Gravel of two different colours picks out the design. The young hedges have yet to reach maturity and join up. Columnar shrubs in the centre of the circles add to the overall effect.

Dwarf box (Buxus sempervirens 'Suffruticosa') forms a tight globe-shaped mound (right). Clip in late spring to promote growth, and trim in summer.

Andrew Lawson

you. Look for one with a chapter or two about knot gardens.

Once you have worked out your plan on paper, it is time to begin in the garden. The first thing to do is to make sure that your site is perfectly level; when you come to lay out your design, lumps and bumps will spoil the final effect.

The contrasting greens of two different types of hedging shrub (above) are set off by two further greens in the central diamond, all against the neutral background of a gravel surround and filling. The initials 'C' and 'E' in the middle have been formed from trimmed box.

The parterre and the knot garden are very similar in concept. The term 'parterre' usually refers to a much larger area of planting, the sort that graces terraces of great houses. The boundary hedge of a parterre is often not square or rectangular and may have 'gateways' leading into the design. This vivid floral design (right) is a section of a parterre.

Tania Midgley

39

There is a lot of choice when it comes to choosing the best hedging plants for the outlines of your knot garden.

Hedges and outlines

A dwarf box, such as *Buxus sempervirens* 'Suffruticosa', makes an excellent, if expensive, choice. It forms a dense mass of bright green, oval leaves and does not mind being regularly clipped.

Santolina chamaecyparissus, known variously as cotton lavender or lavender cotton, is another good choice. The grey-green leaves make a fine foil for colourful flowers and the greens of herbs.

The 'Munstead' variety of lavender has a nice compact shape suitable for edging, hedging and outlining. Once again the grey-green leaves make for an attractive contrast for other, more vibrant shades. Lavender has the added bonus of being scented.

Hyssop (*Hyssopus officinalis*) is an old-fashioned herb that was much loved by the Elizabethans. Its aromatic leaves are a rich, deep green and the blue flowers are very attractive to butterflies, bees and other insects.

An attractive idea is to use one of the grey-green plants to make your overall outline and to use a contrasting colour for the actual knots.

Bold plantings are best between hedges. Even the simplest knot garden is fairly intricate, compared with straightforward beds and borders. If the planting scheme is fussy it will undermine the elegance you are striving for.

Filling the knots

Pansies, pinks, forget-me-nots, polyanthus, nasturtiums and sweet violets are all suitable flowers for a knot garden. Modern bedding plants such as pelargoniums, French marigolds and petunias can also look enchanting if they are gathered into bold groups.

Small knots look best if they are planted with one colour.

The tight planting of this arrangement (right) makes the most of the contrasting colours to produce a pattern of different tones and shapes. The effect is achieved by interplanting low hedges with three herbs, including a purple-leaved sage.

This different style of herb garden (bottom right) uses the varying shapes of several herbs in each diamond to provide the interest. The herbs grown here include tarragon, fennel and rue.

PROJECT

MAKING A TUDOR KNOT

This design dates from 1577. The basic principle of using pegs, string and a bottle of sand can be adapted for any symmetrical, geometric design you choose.

Have your hedging plants ready to plant as soon as your design is laid out, otherwise rain or wind may destroy the sandy outline. Make sure the bed is perfectly smooth and flat.

Plant your hedging plants along the sand trails. Planting distances will vary depending on the hedging you have chosen. Check these carefully as you do not want unsightly gaps when they have matured.

1 *Make a perfectly square bed. Find the exact centre by stretching strings from corner to corner. Place a peg firmly in the ground where they cross.*

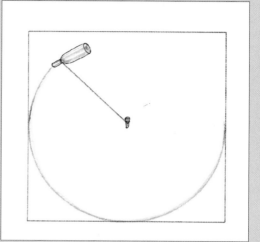

2 *Tie a string to the central peg and, making sure it is fairly taut, attach the end to a bottle of sand. Make a circle by allowing the sand to run out.*

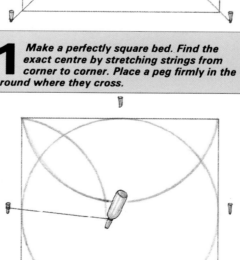

3 *Place a peg halfway along one side of your square and make a semi-circle within the square with the bottle of sand. Repeat on each of the four sides.*

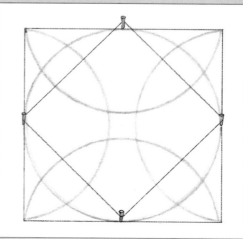

4 *Finally, place pegs at the exact mid-point of each side. Run strings between them to make a diamond shape. Run the sand bottle along the strings.*

Andrew Lawson

Eric Crichton

Larger knots can take two colours or possibly three, if one of them is a silver foliage plant.

Bulbs are also good in a knot garden. Tulips and daffodils were much prized in Elizabethan England and several very old varieties survive to this day. Garden hyacinths will bring scent, colour and a tidy habit to the garden in spring, while the low-growing habit and bold colours of crocuses also look good.

Traditionally, herbs played an important role in the knot garden. These lovely, fragrant plants lend themselves to a formal setting.

You can make your knot garden entirely out of herbs or you can combine them with your favourite bedding plants. Basil, marjoram, rosemary, parsley, pennyroyal, oregano and tarragon, among many others, will provide a fragrant filling for your design.

A USEFUL TOOL

Circles, semi-circles and other 'roundwork' can be tricky, but you can make yourself a useful tool called a bilboquet to help.

Simply tie a peg at one end of a piece of string and make knots along the string at intervals of 20cm/8in. Pegs can be inserted into these knots as required and the bilboquet may be used as a compass to 'draw' your circles and roundwork clearly upon the ground.

SHORT CUTS

Simple Topiary

The training of shrubs to definite shapes is as popular today as it has ever been. You just need a little time and patience to create your own mini masterpiece.

Topiary is a form of sculpture, but you do not have to be a great artist to create your own work of art. All you need is a good eye and a certain amount of patience.

You may have been inspired by seeing large hedges or bushes clipped into impressive shapes in parks and gardens open to the public. It is not necessary, however, to have a large or very grand garden to enjoy topiary because it does not have to be done on such a massive scale. Tiny modern specimens look very much at home in small contemporary gardens.

Easy when you know

To sweep away another misconception, training topiary specimens does not have to be complicated, provided you stick to fairly simple shapes and keep them small. It is best to use evergreen shrubs for topiary and, of course, they must be amenable to regular trimming.

There are several shrubs that are commonly used. The traditional ones include yew (*Taxus baccata*), with its small, very densely packed, dark green needle-like leaves. Yew is fairly slow growing so if you choose this you will need reasonable patience. It will make about 15cm/6in of growth a year.

Choose your plant

Box (*Buxus sempervirens*) has tiny, rounded, glossy green leaves and a similar growth rate to yew.

An excellent choice as a hedge or screen, it is a great

Peter McHoy

Traditionally, yew (Taxus baccata) and box (Buxus sempervirens) are used for topiary. Clipped yews (facing page) are frequently found in formal gardens. For smaller gardens, container grown specimens, like the trained and trimmed box (above), are ideal.

favourite for topiary work because it stands up well to drastic pruning. If left untrimmed, common box will grow to 3m/10ft or more. Smaller varieties which make interesting subjects for topiary include *B. sempervirens* 'Marginata' which has yellow edges to its

leaves and 'Aureovariegata', whose leaves are covered in yellow blotches.

Privets are available in a number of colourful varieties. *Ligustrum vulgare* 'Aureum' has yellow leaves. *L. ovalifolium* 'Aureum', the golden privet, has green leaves edged with yellow, while 'Argentum' has cream-edged leaves.

Honeysuckle is usually thought of as a climbing plant, but Chinese honeysuckle, *Lonicera nitida,* is a shrub that is useful as a hedge or specimen shrub. 'Baggesen's Gold' with its pretty yellow leaves is the most colourful of the varieties .

The small-leaved holly, *Ilex aquifolium* 'Ferox', sometimes called hedgehog holly, is another possibility. It is prickly to handle, though, so be sure to wear gloves.

Topiary specimens can be grown in tubs on a patio. They look good against a background of paving and buildings, providing a good focal

tion, particularly with regard to watering, if grown directly in the ground. Here it can be used to draw the eye to some particular part of the garden. For instance, a topiary specimen can be sited at the end of a lawn, in a corner that needs brightening up or at the bend

GROWING TIPS

HEALTHY GROWTH

Start with young bushy shrubs for topiary work and plant in spring. You want your specimens to be bushy, without gaps. Feeding annually with a flower-garden fertilizer will keep them healthy and watering well in dry weather will ensure steady growth.

This cheeky chap (right) could be a dog or an imaginary creature dreamed up by its creator. Whatever it is, it illustrates the fine detail that can be achieved with the dense foliage of box. A vast range of animal shapes are possible. You could stick to the ever-popular bird shapes or be more adventurous and try a cat, a rabbit or even a kangaroo.

Photos Horticultural

Andrew Lawson

point. They can also be grown in pairs, to flank a front door, gateway or other entrance.

One slight disadvantage of container-grown topiary is the need for regular watering and feeding. There is also a chance that if a specimen is allowed to become too large or top-heavy, the container might topple over or be blown over in high winds. To avoid this, keep the shape compact, well balanced and, if possible, taper it towards the top.

Topiary needs less atten-

in a path.

Topiary also looks good actually set in a lawn. If you do this, remember not to allow grass to grow right up to it or growth will be retarded: leave a circle of bare soil around the base of the specimen.

What shape to choose?

Most topiary shapes tend to be somewhat rounded and the plants which are most suitable have a naturally bushy, rounded habit.

Animals and birds tend to be

Shrubby Chinese honeysuckle, available with green or yellow leaves, can be trimmed into quite dainty and elegant shapes such as this attractive group of birds (above), which look very much at home in this front garden flower bed.

the most popular shapes: chickens, ducks, peacocks, squirrels, cats and dogs for example, are all firm favourites. If you want something a bit more unusual, why not consider a fish or a frog.

Simple geometric shapes like cubes, pyramids, domes, cones, globes and multiple globes (one above the other on a stem) are also fairly standard, and associate particularly well with modern buildings and very formal surroundings.

When choosing your plant, first bear in mind its natural

shape. As a general guide, yew and box, being very neat in appearance, are particularly recommended for geometric shapes. As they are slow-growing, they are also best for small specimens. For quickly building up more complex shapes, use faster-growing plants, such as privet or Chinese honeysuckle.

Keep it small

Regarding the size of your specimen, do not be too ambitious. For very tiny gardens aim for around 60cm/24in in height. In a larger garden the size could be increased to about 1.2–1.5m/4–5ft.

It is best to use one plant per topiary specimen, rather than trying to speed the process by planting several (if one should die the effect will be ruined).

The simpler the shape the easier training will be. The simplest are the basic geometric shapes. It is advisable to wait until your plant has become established before you

Eric Crichton

Andrew Lawson

Because it is constantly growing, topiary can be changed and modified. Here is a topiary dog sitting on a ball (above). On either side of the dog shape, two clumps are being encouraged to develop and these will be trimmed into a pair of puppies.

This large terracotta pot (left) forms a sturdy base for a streamlined duck formed from box. Consider colour as well as shape: here the soil's surface is covered with a layer of gravel to form a light-coloured background in clear contrast to the deep green leaves.

GARDEN NOTES

TIME TO TRIM

Small-leaved shrubs like those recommended here should be trimmed with garden shears. Late spring is a good time, with further trimmings during the summer for vigorous specimens. Light trimming, just removing shoot tips, is the rule with topiary, whether training or maintaining completed specimens.

PRETTY PATIOS

It is not necessary to grow topiary specimens in tubs for decorating a patio. Why not remove a paving slab or two and plant direct in the soil? First remove any rubble and fill the hole with good garden soil. Mulch with gravel or bark to help preserve moisture.

Here is a quirky idea: an armchair that no one can sit in! Though its shape looks comfortable and inviting, it is made from yellow privet and is for decoration only.

Andrew Lawson

Harry Smith

Topiary is most effective in a formal setting. This elegant spiral column forms an eye-catching corner-piece to a bed of low rose bushes, adding shape and height. Its contours can be seen clearly against the light-coloured background of a path made from paving slabs and gravel.

choose the shape of your topiary specimen. You may find it impossible to form a peacock shape, say, from a bush that would rather grow into the form of a rabbit.

Once you have decided upon your shape, you will need to form the basic outline using wire. Use stiff galvanized wire to describe the main lines. This 'former', as it is called, should be positioned as firmly as possible. You may find it necessary to hold it in place with bamboo canes inserted into the soil.

At first the former will contain the plant but it will eventually be hidden completely by foliage. Once your specimen is well established, the wires can be removed, if you wish. If you decide to leave them in place, however, make sure that the wire does not cut into the wood or strangle the branches. Take care when trimming, too, or you may blunt your shears.

A regular trim

With topiary it is important to trim the shrub regularly as it grows – at least once a year, preferably more for vigorous growers. Young shrubs are best lightly trimmed on a regular basis before they grow beyond the formers, as this will ensure really dense

P ROJECT   AN IVY BIRD

Here is a quick and easy way of creating topiary specimens with evergreen ivy. Choose a climbing, small-leaved ivy – *Hedera helix* is ideal.

Green-leaved ivies are extremely hardy and can be grown anywhere, including shady spots. Variegated and yellow varieties are not quite so hardy and could have their leaves damaged by frost or wind during winter.

Buy ivies which have been specially grown for use as climbers. In garden centres they will be tied upright to bamboo canes. Bear in mind that ivy will take a year to settle down, making little top growth. But after that it will start to grow vigorously.

Once established, trim ivy topiary with secateurs. Trimming the tips of side shoots will encourage more shoots to form. Every spring, trim growth back but do not cut into the main stems. This may make the specimen look rather bald for a few weeks but new foliage will soon be produced.

Ray Duns

1 *Create a framework with wire netting. Hold the framework in place with a thick bamboo cane.*

growth with plenty of shoots being produced. To begin, though, allow the leading shoot to grow erect until the required height is reached, then remove its tip. You may need to tie some shoots into the former while they are still flexible – it all depends on the shape you are aiming for.

If you are put off by the idea of using a former, you can simply trim your plant as it grows, using your eyes as a guide. Some stems may need training to a particular shape and this can be done by spiralling a length of plastic-covered wire around them and bending them into the shape that is required.

Alternatively you may be able to tie stems in place with string. Once they are capable of retaining this shape on their own, the wire or string can be carefully removed.

It is not always necessary to

Geoff Dann/Garden Picture Library

> **SHORT CUTS**
>
> ### QUICK TO GROW
> Quick-growing shrubs suitable for topiary include oval-leaf privet (*Ligustrum ovalifolium*) and its golden form, both with small oval leaves, and the Chinese honeysuckle (*Lonicera nitida*) and its golden variety, 'Baggesen's Gold', with tiny oval leaves. Both shrubs should produce up to 30cm/12in of growth annually.

Set each plant in a hole slightly deeper than the rootball so that it is only just covered with soil.

3 *Set the plants as close as possible to the cane. Space out the stems and tie in place.*

A topiary tortoise (left) made from shrubby honeysuckle, is an easy shape to achieve, while a basket like this one (above), though quite straightforward, will take a little more time, effort and skill. Make the basic basket shape, with or without a handle, from box or privet. Leave a hollow centre in which you can place a pot containing a plant with a contrasting leaf colour or even some bright flowers.

start from scratch. You may already have a hedge or bush in your garden that is in need of some attention. The obvious way of taming a straggly hedge is to trim it to a neat, rectangular outline, but why not try to do something a bit different? Be creative! Give your imagination free rein.

Handsome hedges
Letting the shape of the hedge or bush guide you, try creating waves or zigzags, a serpent or a whole row of ducks or fish.

If you make a mistake or are not pleased with the finished results, do not despair. Your hedge or bush will keep growing and the shape can be altered slightly each time you trim it. Remember, whatever it is you are creating is not something static: this is *living* sculpture.

The Cottage Garden

Bring a touch of the countryside to your garden with an informal bank of cottage-style blooms, and have a flower-filled display all summer.

Insight Picture Library

Select old-fashioned favourites (roses).

Let plants spread, providing ground cover.

You don't have to live in a thatched cottage to copy the 'look' of a cottage garden, with its overflowing beds of pretty, perfumed flowers. The cottage garden look is something you can achieve wherever you live and whatever the size of your garden.

You may not want to change the look of your whole garden, but you could choose a few cottage-garden plants that appeal to you and devote a small area of your garden to them, or simply add them to your existing flower beds. As well as looking pretty, a mixture of scented species near the house can fill the air with a wonderful heady fragrance on summer evenings. In a real pocket handkerchief sized plot, you can create a very authentic cottage garden look just by filling every scrap of space with flowers and you will find that this weed-smothering style is easy to maintain.

What is a cottage garden?

Centuries ago, a typical cottage garden would have been very different to our image of it today. A 'real' cottage garden would have been more like a smallholding; with vegetables, herbs, fruit trees and livestock — hens, ducks and geese, rabbits and a pig or perhaps even a cow. Flowers — if there were any — would have been limited mainly to wild plants that found their way in from the surrounding countryside. Basically, the true cottage garden would have looked a bit of a mess!

By Victorian times the 'cottage garden' had become very fashionable, and the typical example bore little relation to its original predecessor.

Today's cottage garden is likely to be a charming and rather disorderly blend of flowers and herbs spilling over brick or gravel paths and daisy-studded grass, with plants arranged to give a wild, natural look as though the garden just 'happened'.

Old-fashioned roses

A cottage garden relies on a mixture of flowers, including roses, for its effect. While modern varieties of rose can look perfectly in keeping in a cottage garden, if you really want to be authentic it pays to choose the sort that are nowadays called old-fashioned. A modern hybrid tea rose, for example, would never look right, but an old-fashioned, rambling

Plant with a wall, fence or hedge as background.

Stately giants, like delphiniums, need staking.

Plant close together, in small groups.

Tall plants don't have to be set at the back

FOR YOUR OWN GARDEN

This rather grand cottage garden can easily be scaled down to fit a smaller patch; the basic structure of a cottage garden is the same whether for a stately home or your back garden. Using the ideas given here you can copy the style to transform as much or as little of your garden as you wish.

Use patches of white to offset strong colours.

Choose perennials or plants that self-seed (sweet William).

Include dainty flowers (aquilegia) as well as the bolder types.

Some plants can be left to sprawl happily (catmint).

A mixture (right) of sweet William, campion, crane's bill, daisy-like chrysanthemums, pansies and cornflowers provides a profusion of small-petalled blooms.
Having such a packed flower bed not only fills the garden with colour, but has the added advantage of suppressing weed growth.

Eric Crichton

As beautiful indoors as out – a selection (below) of sweet peas, pansies, miniature roses and cosmos in shades of pastel pink, white and burgundy, informally arranged in a jug.

Jonathan Alden

finished blooming.

If it is important to you to have plants with a long flowering season, then choose bourbon or hybrid perpetual roses. These varieties can be relied on to produce flowers, albeit gradually fewer, during the later summer months and into autumn after the main flush of flower is over.

Essential plants

Although a mixture of different plants is an important factor of the cottage garden look, some plants are a 'must' and almost guarantee the romantic effect you are trying to achieve. Delphiniums, poppies, foxgloves, wallflowers, columbine and pot marigolds are prime examples.

Another 'classic' component of the cottage garden is a climber. This will give an appropriate look of unruliness and fullness to your cottage garden bed or border. Pretty examples are winter jasmine, climbing roses or honeysuckle. Train any one of these on to a wall, fence or trellis, or around the front door or porch. Clematis, too, has a suitably random appearance, and grows at an astonishing and satisfying rate. You may prefer to train one of these climbers over an arch made from wood or wire for a truly rustic effect.

Fruit and vegetables

Fruit trees – especially apples – always had a place in a real cottage garden. Nowadays

rose with delicate, flat-faced, pale-toned flowers would be ideal. Old-fashioned roses have the added advantage of usually being quite strongly perfumed.

Old-fashioned roses are easy to grow. They rarely need pruning, and suffer much less from disease than modern varieties. They have a shorter flowering period than hybrid teas however: sometimes only four to six weeks in the middle of summer. This is why they are usually grown amongst other old-fashioned flowers, chosen specially to carry on flowering when the roses have

---

Garden Notes

LOW MAINTENANCE VALUE

Many cottage garden plants are natural self-seeders, so you can let them do the work of re-stocking for you. After a little while you will have a carpet of densely packed flowers. If the garden begins to look too crowded or if plants pop up in the wrong place, simply thin them out where they are not welcome. The following are particularly good self-seeders:

Alyssum (madwort)
Aquilegia (columbine)
Campanula (bellflower)
Centranthus (valerian)
Helleborus (Christmas rose)

Lavatera (mallow)
Linaria (toadflax)
Myosotis (forget-me-not)
Papaver (poppy)

PROJECT PLANTING PLAN FOR A COTTAGE GARDEN BORDER

W A L L

climbers · climbers · tall shrub · tall perennial · large spreading shrub · tall shrub · tall perennial · self-seeded plants · medium perennial · self-seeded plants · medium perennial · tall perennial · wild flowers · wild flowers · wild flowers · self-seeded plants · self-seeded flowers · medium annuals · self-seeded plants · herb · low growing spreading plant · scented flowers · low growing herb · edging plants · edging plants

Julia Bigg

P A T H

Climbers –clematis, climbing rose, fan-trained fig, apricot, peach or apple tree
Edging plants – dwarf box, lavender, thyme, London pride
Large spreading shrubs – lavatera (mallow), *Viburnum fragrans*, lilac, azaleas, hydrangea
Low-growing herbs – thyme, marjoram
Low-growing spreading plants – *Stachys lanata* 'Silver Carpet' (lamb's ears)
Medium annuals – busy Lizzie (impatiens), petunia, salvia
Medium perennials – *Alchemilla mollis* (lady's mantle), ornamental grass, astrantia (masterwort)
Scented flowers – night scented stock, tobacco plant (nicotiana), dianthus (pinks)
Self-seeders – forget-me-not, poppies, aquilegia, foxgloves, honesty, nasturtiums, marigolds
Tall perennials – echinops (globe thistle), delphinium, lily, lupin, foxgloves, hollyhock
Tall shrubs – *Ribes sanguineum* (flowering currant), *Hamamelis mollis* (Chinese witch hazel)
Wild flowers – cornflowers, geranium (crane's-bill), foxglove

The plan (above) is an example of how you could plant up a flower bed for a cottage garden look. A list of suitable plants is given, left. The ideal depth for this flower bed is 1.2-1.5m/4-5ft.

gardeners tend to plant them not only for fruit, but for the spring blossom and as supports for climbers which scramble up through their branches. Again, really old varieties with evocative names like 'Devonshire Quarrenden', 'D'Arcy Spice' and 'Cornish Aromatic' are still occasionally available from specialist growers. Though not heavy croppers, the flavour of these apples is truly delicious – far better than most fruit you buy from the supermarket.

Vegetables – the mainstay of real old cottage gardens – don't have to make the place look like an allotment. They can be grown in your border, mixed in with the flowers, where they look most attractive. When vegetables are grown to eat, it is the fruit of the plant that is all-important, but they often have interesting foliage and flowers too.

Try scarlet runner beans or climbing pea varieties growing on a wigwam of rustic bean-poles at the back of a flower bed; globe artichokes along-side delphiniums; or an edging of parsley or thyme by a path.

Romantic disorder

The essence of the traditional, romantic cottage garden is its overcrowded look, with plants filling every bit of space and spilling out over paths and grass. In the past, this look took many years to achieve – largely as a result of neglect! Nowadays we tend to create a more orderly version of the same look, with the emphasis on carefully selected cottage garden plants. Invasive plants still have their place – they are best grown together in a bed of their own where they make an ideal low-maintenance cottage border. The most important beds, however, or those where growing conditions are best, should be reserved for the less pushy plants which can then grow quite safely without risk

PERFECT PARTNERS

Ann Kelly/The Garden Picture Library

A vibrant and daring mixture of reds (lupins and sweet William), pink (peonies) and purple (campanula) creates an unusually striking effect.

of suffocation. If choice plants happen to self-seed, then you can think yourself lucky and either leave them where they fall or transplant them to another part of the garden.

Attractive combinations

Having decided which kinds of plants you want to grow, the next trick is deciding how to

Harry Smith Collection

Same family, different flower: the gladioli in the main picture (below) are an old-fashioned species, G. byzantinus, with delicate flowers and a wild look which suits the cottage garden style; whereas a modern hybrid (left) would look out of place with its huge red blooms.

out of hand. The main chores include snipping off dead flowers and cutting back dead or dying stems, pruning, feeding and watering (especially if you have plants in containers) and mulching between plants with garden compost.

The reason for snipping back (deadheading) the dead flowers is to encourage further

David Russell/The Garden Picture Library — *Harry Smith Collection.*

put them together, making pleasant contrasts of shape, texture and colour throughout the summer.

A typical small cottage border in a fairly sunny situation might, for instance, contain some old-fashioned roses, lavender, irises, several different kinds of hardy cranesbills, a few salvias and perhaps some summer flowering bulbs like allium or lilies.

For late summer and early autumn flowers, there might

also be a clump or two of Japanese anemones and some Michaelmas daisies.

Roses and honeysuckle make an attractive partnership and, next to them, you could plant night-scented stock or nicotiana for truly wonderful perfumed evenings.

Easy maintenance

Cottage gardens need little work to maintain: just some sensible clearing from time to time when things start getting

Bumble-bees (inset), along with other nectar-loving insects, will be keen visitors to a flower-filled garden of 'wild' species.

flowering. A plant's purpose in life is to flower, set seed, then die. If you take off the dead flowers before they can seed, you are, in effect, frustrating this course of events, and forcing the plant to try again with new flowers.

If you grow tall flowers, like delphiniums, they will need tying loosely and unobtrusively to canes or stakes to keep their stems straight, but most cottage flowers look more natural if they flop gently.

Harmonizing Yellows *and* Blues

Imitate the best nature has to offer – fill your garden with harmonious shades of blue and yellow, the brilliant colours of summer.

Gillian Beckett

Blue and yellow form one of the happiest colour combinations in any garden. Blue is reminiscent of summer skies, cool shade and still waters. It has a calming effect and is very restful to the eye, while yellow, the sunshine colour, is warm and cheerful.

Although there are few true blue flowers, there are many delightful shades to choose from – from the palest of sky blues to the richness of royal and cobalt blue.

Yellow comes in countless shades, including cream, soft and bright yellows, buff, ochre, golden and acid yellows.

The two colours can be used together to create some very exciting effects in the garden, but be careful not to base your entire design on sharp contrasts.

Bright splashes
For best effect, most of your garden should be composed of a harmonious blend of hues with just the odd splash of strong, bright colour to catch the eye. Before you get down to planning your blue and yellow garden it is worth spending some time studying the way in which these two colours relate to one another. Browse through books and magazines to see how they are combined in fashion and interior design, or take a stroll through show gardens or a natural landscape, looking out for these colours. You can probably even learn from your neighbours' successes or mistakes.

You may like to carry this

Few colours combine to such stunning effect as blue and yellow. This vibrant forsythia 'Spectabilis' is distinctly defined against a clear blue sky. Colours often mingle with their surroundings but these colours retain their identity perfectly. The yellow exudes life, sunshine and excitement and the blue is tranquil.

53

PICK OF THE BLUES

Of all the blue-flowered plants available, here are some of the best from which to make your choice.

glory of the snow (*Chionodoxa* species)	winter and spring-flowering bulbs for a sunny position, 15cm/6in high
pansy (*Viola* species)	winter and spring-flowering annuals or biennials for sun or half shade
forget-me-not (*Myosotis* species)	small spring-flowering biennials for either sun or shade
periwinkle (*Vinca* species)	dwarf spring-flowering, evergreen shrubs for sun or shade
California lilac (*Ceanothus* species)	early summer- or autumn-flowering shrubs for a position in full sun
delphiniums	tall summer-flowering perennials that like sun
lobelia (*L. erinus*)	dwarf summer-flowering edging plants for a sunny spot
African lily (*Agapanthus* species)	late summer-flowering perennials, growing to 60cm/2ft high

Golden rod (above) is a hardy perennial with profuse, yellow flowers. Easy to grow, it will quickly give a blast of radiant colour. Blue and yellow in a flower bed can be breathtaking (right). The tulips (Tulipa fosteriana 'Candela') open up their cups to the sun while the grape hyacinth forms a sea of colour.

Blue flowers come in all shapes and sizes. For a showy display choose delphiniums (left). Their towering spikes can be tinged with pink or purple but most stunning of all is the intense pure blue. In contrast, the tiny glory of the snow, Chionodoxa sardensis (below), only grows to 15cm/6in but makes a beautiful addition to any rock garden.

Vaughan Fleming/Garden Picture Library

Photos Horticultural

Flowering at the end of the winter, the tiny winter aconite, Eranthis hyemalis (above left), adds the first touch of spring colour to your garden. The chrysanthemum 'Charm' (above right) is very much a summer plant however. Plant it in tubs to display on your patio and you will be able to bring them inside for a yellow colour theme indoors over the winter.

While many blue flowers are small and delicate the Californian lilac, Ceanothus impressus, (below) grows to 3m/10ft. As it is used to warmer climates, grow it in a sheltered spot; against a wall is ideal. Clusters of deep blue flowers appear in spring and remain until early summer.

David Squire

PICK OF THE YELLOWS

Yellow flowers abound. Here is a selection of shrubs and perennials that are guaranteed to give good value for money.

winter aconite (*Eranthis hyemalis*)	a winter-flowering perennial perfect for a semi-shaded position, 10cm/4in high
witch hazel (*Hamamelis mollis*)	a large, winter-flowering deciduous shrub that thrives in half-shade
gold dust (*Alyssum saxatile*)	a spring-flowering, sun-loving perennial, 30cm/12in high. Thrives in any ordinary well-drained garden soil.
forsythia (*F. × intermedia*)	a group of large, spring-flowering deciduous shrubs that like full sun
shrubby cinquefoil (*Potentilla* species)	small, early summer-flowering deciduous shrubs for sun or half-shade
broom (*Cytisus battandieri*)	a large, summer-flowering semi-evergreen shrub for a sunny spot
evening primrose (*Oenothera* species)	summer-flowering, sun-loving hardy perennials, from 15-120cm/6-48in high
golden rod (*Solidago* species)	late summer-flowering perennials for a sunny spot, 90cm/36in high

garden colour scheme into your house – it can be extremely effective. Imagine a room which is decorated in pale yellow and rich shades of blue, opening out into a glorious garden full of delicate yellow snapdragons, marigolds, and day lilies, accented by the towering blue spikes of delphiniums. The effect would be positively stunning!

Select a shade

Once you have an idea of those shades of blue and yellow you would like to use, it is time to select a dominant colour for your scheme. You can either choose one for the whole year or pick a different colour for each season.

In spring, for example, you may like to use lots of bright, cheerful yellows to herald the arrival of a new year. There are plenty of yellow spring flowers to choose from, all of which contrast beautifully with forget-me-nots, scilla and other blue flowers of spring.

Bright blues in summer echo the clear, sunny skies. In autumn, shades of gold, bronze and grey-blues complement the muted, earthy colours typical of this time of year.

Once you have chosen your dominant colour theme for each season, you need to combine each with various other shades of blue and yellow to create a pleasing overall effect.

NATURAL BEAUTY

Blue and yellow flowers abound in natural settings: just think of woods thickly carpeted with bluebells in springtime, and lush green hedgerows dotted with pale yellow primroses.

If you have the space in your garden, why not create your own wildflower patch, using blue and yellow as your theme?
- In a grassy area, blue cornflowers (*Centaurea cyanus*), yellow corn marigolds (*Chrysanthemum segetum*), common toadflax (*Linaria vulgaris*) and meadow buttercups (*Ranunculus acris*) can all be grown from seed, simply scattered in autumn where you want the flowers to appear the following year.
- In a shady, wooded area, the bluebell is really at home. (In fact, the more light it receives, the less intense the colour.) Partner it with yellow archangel (*Lamium galeobdolon*), a dead nettle with bright yellow flower spikes.
- For an area of damp semi-shade, blue bugle is at home with pale yellow primroses, sunny lesser celandine and intense blue germander speedwell (*Veronica chamaedrys*).

A blue and yellow combination often occurs naturally. These hyacinths and tulips form a bright spot in a dull landscape.

These cheerful pansies (right) look gloriously happy when planted in such a wonderful colour combination. The blue makes the lemon yellow seem more vivid while the yellow in turn enhances the purply-blue pansy, drawing attention to the tiny spot of yellow at the centre of its pretty face. They enjoy any fertile, well-drained soil and you can keep them flowering by regularly removing the dead flower-heads.

Andrew Lawson

Marije Heuff/Garden Picture Library

Blue and yellow can be used to create a wild and unruly effect. The border (left) has been carefully planned to combine blue and yellow plants of varying shades and heights, but the effect is casually charming. Cranesbill (geranium), delphiniums, irises, tall limey-yellow euphorbia and pretty little pansies complete the picture.

Blues and yellows can also be used to create a more simple and formal look (below). Tall, medium and short plants have been planted in military rows but the flowers refuse to be regimented. The deep yellow tickseed, Coreopsis lanceolata, forms a sunny edge. A row of salvia breaks up the blue and yellow, with spikes of stately delphiniums at the back.

The colours you choose should enhance one another rather than detract. For instance, pale yellow and dark blue make a more striking combination than gold and pale blue.

Use soft, muted shades blended together for swathes of soft colour, as well as for softening the effects of strong or bright colours. These will create a warm, restful effect. Be sure to make each patch of subtle colour big enough to hold its own among the splashes of brighter colours.

Dark or strong colours need to be used with care or they will soon overpower your colour scheme. Use them in small amounts as exclamation points in the garden. As a rule of thumb, it is better to let lighter colours dominate darker ones, and weaker colours dominate strong ones.

Soft shades of clear colours

Eric Crichton

look marvellous massed in large drifts. Misty shades of pastel yellows and blues form an almost dream-like garden setting. You may, on the other hand, prefer to make a bold statement, filling the garden with bright, vibrant colours and contrasts.

Whatever combination of blue and yellow you choose, do not forget to consider the background against which your display will be viewed. Deep green evergreens make a superb background for the various shades of yellow. The paler greens of deciduous shrubs look good behind yellow and blue flowers, but check that their autumn colour does not clash with your colour theme.

Complete harmony

It is also important that your colour scheme should harmonize with its surroundings. Buildings, patios, paths, fences and walls are all part of the final picture, but cannot easily be changed. Garden furniture, pots and containers, however, can be chosen with the blue and yellow colour scheme in mind. Paint fences and gates in a harmonious shade of blue or yellow – or just clean, crisp, brilliant white – to fit in with your theme.

Blue and yellow makes the best use of sun and shade conditions in your garden. Blue will have a cooling effect in a hot, sunny border while yellow can be used to add a splash of colour to a shady area.

INSTANT COLOUR

Fill the spaces in your borders with bedding plants for bright splashes of colour.

For yellows, choose Californian poppies, French and African marigolds and snapdragons, begonias, chrysanthemums and tobacco plants.

For touches of blue, try love-in-a-mist or annual delphiniums.

SHORT CUTS

All-white Borders

Using white-flowered plants and those with creamy white or silver foliage in your garden give it a feeling of extra space and a sense of calm.

White flowers and silvery foliage can be used in many ways to produce glistening and gleaming effects. During the day, white provides a strong focus; as the sun surrenders to the evening twilight, white and silver accents gleam like bright moonlight.

Strictly speaking, white is neither a colour nor the absence of colour. In fact, it is all the colours of the spectrum present at the same time. As a result, it enhances and enlivens those colours with which it is combined.

White flowers will, by contrast, deepen the dominant colour of a bed or border. They also act to defuse and cool down hot colours that might be too brash to get on well together. Even a narrow drift of white between the colours will put a surprising amount of space between two inharmonious or harsh colours.

Plants with grey and silver foliage also work well as buffers between clashing colours. When combined with white flowers, they add to the shimmering effect.

White drifts

The effect of white is best seen if a white area is enclosed or otherwise separated from the rest of the garden. Make the entrance to a white garden as narrow as possible. When you step through it, you will be instantly struck by the sense of space created by the combination of white and green.

Of course, few gardens have space for an enclosed garden of any size. Fortunately, white

S & O Mathews

A pure white garden is perhaps beyond the scope of most people, but there is no denying the effect of white flowers against green foliage (above). Here, the pure white rose, Rosa 'Iceberg', is planted with white valerian.

Foliage plants also contribute to an overall 'white' look. Artemisia ludoviciana albula (right) has soft, grey, woolly leaves which complement the plumes of dainty summer flowers.

The tiny, white double flowers of Gypsophila paniculata dissolve into a cloud when seen from even a short distance (far right). Here, it is planted with the pale, wispy, lavender-coloured flowers of nepeta.

Harry Smith Collection

Photos Horticultural

> **GARDEN NOTES**
>
> ## MAINTENANCE
>
> The disadvantage of an all-white garden is that the flowers fade and discolour to a smudgy brown, making for a rather grubby and unattractive overall look. Avoid this by dead-heading on a daily basis and especially after rain.

can also be used to good effect in borders of mixed hues, creating a deeper colour range and acting as a buffer between strong colours.

Many plants suit this role. The flowers of a white achillea such as *A. ptarmica* 'The Pearl' stand so strongly apart from its foliage that you hardly notice it. It grows to 75cm/2½ft and spreads quickly to form clumps. On a summer evening, its numerous small white flowers dance like tiny stars through the garden.

Another favourite is the small-flowered perennial gypsophila (*G. paniculata* 'Bristol Fairy'). Once again, the flowers dominate by sheer force of numbers, despite the small size of the blooms.

Everlasting pearl (*Anaphalis margaritacea*) and the white variety of rose campion (*Lychnis coronaria* 'Alba') are useful for the middle and front of a border. Both have soft, velvety-textured silver leaves and white heads of attractive summer flowers.

For the back of a border, choose a white foxglove (*Digitalis purpurea* 'Alba'). It may be difficult to buy as a plant, but seed is available and its tall, elegant spires of pure white flowers make a delightful contribution to a drift of white in the border.

Edges

White's ability to separate areas of colour and interest makes it a particularly useful colour at the edges of a bed or a border, where low-growing white or silver plants really

The flowers of **Achillea ptarmica** *'The Pearl' – also known as 'Boule de Neige' – (above) make up in numbers what they lack in size.*

RECOMMENDED VARIETIES

Plant	Description	Season
Perennials		
Achillea ptarmica 'The Pearl'	Clusters of white flowers. Spreads quickly	Summer
Everlasting pearl (*Anaphalis margaritacea*)	Silver foliage, clusters of white flowers	Late summer
Artemisia (*Artemisia ludoviciana albula*)	Silver, aromatic leaves. Grey-white flowers.	Summer
Dianthus 'Mrs Sinkins'	Old-fashioned pink with white flowers and silver foliage.	Spring/ Summer
Foxglove (*Digitalis purpurea* 'Alba')	Short-lived perennials with tubular white flowers.	Summer
Gypsophila paniculata 'Bristol Fairy'	Small, double white flowers	Summer
Lychnis coronaria 'Alba'	Silver stems and leaves; white flowers	Mid-late summer
Senecio maritima (syn. Cineraria maritima) 'Silver Dust' & 'Cirrhus'	Silver foliage; half-hardy.	All year
Annuals		
Sweet alyssum (*Alyssum maritima* 'Little Dorrit')	Greyish leaves, small, white, scented flowers.	Summer to autumn
Matthiola 'Giant Imperial'	Greyish leaves, creamy white scented flowers	Spring/ summer

Neil Holmes

Photos Horticultural

S & O Mathews

White is a good background, throwing colours forward (above). Here, the full blooms of Rosa 'Iceberg' and the pendent panicles of Russian vine (Polygonum baldschuanicum) set off a bed of dahlias.

Among the several paradoxically white varieties of pink, Dianthus 'Mrs Sinkins' (far left) stands out for purity of colour.

Varieties of Hydrangea paniculata *(left) have white flower-heads that are conical in shape rather than the more familiar dome shape.*

Helichrysum petiolare, also known as H. petiolatum, forms mounds of grey-green foliage from which spring pale cream summer flower-heads. It is best used in a container, as here, or as edging for a border.

come into their own.

For edging beds with silver, the traditional choice is senecio (*Senecio maritima*), with its deeply-cut, soft-textured leaves. Both 'Silver Dust' and 'Cirrhus' are useful contrast plants though, because of its low-growing habit, 'Silver Dust' is more often used as an edging or bedding plant.

Artemisias provide silver foliage for the middle and back of the border. *Artemisia ludoviciana albula* offers silver leaves and tiny, grey-white flowers in summer. It grows to about 1.2m/4ft in height, flopping in a lax way as it spreads, but this increases its usefulness as a barrier plant.

Silver carpets
One of the most useful silver foliage plants is *Helichrysum petiolare*. Its soft-textured, silvery-white leaves are carried on arching stems that trail attractively over the edges when planted in a container. It is also used as an edging plant in a mixed border or as mound-forming ground cover. The foliage is complemented by small, creamy flowers in summer.

Snow-in-summer (*Cerastium tomentosum*) combines greyish leaves with small white flowers to make a dense ground cover; it will smother a dry, sunny bank with a flush of silver and white. It is also a good rockery plant and tumbles attractively over the sides

of tall terracotta containers. One of its most useful roles is as ground cover at the base of an evergreen conifer hedge.

Rose choice
White roses are probably the most popular plants of any white feature in a garden. There are many pure whites, but the best choice is perhaps *Rosa* 'Iceberg'. It produces clusters of cupped, double flowers, and can be used as a bush rose or, in its climbing form, against a trellis or up a pillar. It flowers from summer through to autumn.

Many white-flowered shrubs will provide waves of blooms in season, but, once flowering is over, their green foliage will dominate. Hydrangeas, viburnum, lilac and the butterfly bush (*Buddleia davidii*) all have lovely white forms that will make a bold and attractive show in season.

The mock orange (*Philadelphus* spp.) is popular for its densely packed white flowers, redolent of orange blossom, which are borne on graceful arching stems against glossy foliage; try planting *P.* 'Belle Etoile' or, for double flowers, *P.* 'Boule d'Argent'.

Many species of daisy bush have a happy combination of white flowers and silver foliage. They suit a mixed border or can be used as white accents against a shed or near the house. Both *Olearia virgata* – which can grow to 6m/20ft

WHITE CONTAINERS
The principles of white planting can be applied, scaled down, to a basket or window box. Use *Helichrysum petiolare* as a basic foliage plant to give shape and texture to your container. Allow white-flowererd lobelia to trail over the edges. For the middle of the container use white varieties of pansy or petunia. White-flowered pelargoniums will give height to a hanging basket, which can also benefit from a variegated ivy twining around its chains.

– and the more contained *O. mollis* (1m/3ft) have dense heads of white, daisy-like flowers that are set off well by their attractive silvery-grey or grey-green leaves.

Small shrubs
With its yellow-centred, white trumpet flowers and silvery-green leaves, *Convolvulus cneorum* is a perfect choice as a small specimen shrub. Frost-hardy, and growing to a height and spread of 1m/3ft, it suits a sunny, well-drained, mixed shrub and perennial border. It will also make an attractive year-round buffer in your colour scheme.

Smaller and equally well-suited to a dry, sunny site is *Dorycnium hirsutum*, a bushy

Gillian Beckett

BEATING THE BIRDS
The soft texture of silver leaves and white flowers is attractive to nesting sparrows and other birds in spring. They may strip plants bare of foliage and young shoots. Protect the plants with cages of cotton wound round canes, or use silver foil bird scarers until nesting is over and the plants well-established.

GROWING TIPS

Derek Gould

Brigitte Thomas/Garden Picture Library

A WHITE BULB GARDEN

You can enjoy a succession of white flowers from bulbous plants through the year, beginning with the early spring crocus, *Crocus sieberi* 'Bowles' White' or 'Alba'. Other spring bulbs, such as tulips, narcissus, grape hyacinth and of course snowdrops all come in white and creamy forms. The spring star flower (*Ipheion uniflorum*) is usually blue, but a white variety will add style and charm.

In summer, lilies – including the Madonna lily – gladioli and camassia bring unusual shapes and flower forms to the bulb garden (right), followed by the appearance of white autumn crocus (*Colchicum speciosum* 'Album'). Winter white comes from varieties of *Cyclamen coum*.

Michael Shoebridge

The large (12cm/5in across) flowers of Clematis 'Henryi' (above left) provide bold areas of well-defined white at the height of summer.

Dorycnium hirsutum (right) is a low-growing (60cm/24in) shrub whose silver-edged leaves make it a good choice for a white garden; the pink flush on the flower buds gives way as they open to a pure white flower.

62

PERFECT PARTNERS

Gillian Beckett

Silver plants make a wonderful background foil for pink or red flowers, deepening the red tones. Use artemisias behind and around pink roses, or next to penstemons or diascia (above).

The tortuous branches of the woody climber **Wisteria floribunda** *'Alba' provide interest even in the winter months, when the pale green leaves have gone, but the plant is in its full glory in early summer (above), when long, white racemes of sweetly-scented white flowers drip from its gracefully arching branches.*

Photos Horticultural

plant with silky-textured silver-grey leaves. In summer, its pinkish-white buds open to white, pea-like flowers.

White climbers

White-flowered climbing plants grown on trellis extensions above boundary walls or against the back wall of the house offer a sense of extra space and height. Many have the added attraction of fragrant flowers.

White wisteria (*Wisteria sinensis* 'Alba') grows at least 6m/20ft on each spreading stem. Its vanilla-scented pea-like flowers hang in long trails in early summer. For a pergola, choose white Japanese wisteria (*W. floribunda* 'Alba').

Several clematis provide seasonal successions of white flowers to grace your patio walls. In a protected, sunny position, grow the evergreen white clematis (*C. armandii*), with scented early spring flowers. For mid-season white use *Clematis* 'Henryi' and for late summer flowers choose *Clematis flammula*.

Standing alone

Well-shaped specimen trees or shrubs make very useful large white accents in a garden. If you have the space for a good-sized tree, the white-flowered cherry (*Prunus avium* 'Plena') offers clouds of double white

flowers all through the spring. It can reach up to 12m/40ft.

Smaller, but equally generous with their spring flowers, are two other cherries, *P.* 'Mount Fuji' and *P.* 'Tai Haku'. They form round heads and can reach 8m/24ft.

One of the most unusual white-flowering trees is a dogwood (*Cornus controversa* 'Variegata') known as the wedding cake tree because of its tiered branches. At its mature height of 8m/24ft it makes a very full crown. However, the combination of delicate, white summer flowers and creamy white variegated leaves give it a light and airy appearance.

Silver threads

For a similar effect in silvery-grey, use weeping pear (*Pyrus salicifolia* 'Pendula'). In full sun, it grows to a height and spread of up to 10m/30ft, half that in a small garden. It has small white spring flowers and weeping branches that sweep the ground, making an informal hedge-like mound.

Variegated, silver-edged forms of holly also produce sparkling effects, especially when they are caught by rays of winter sunlight. *Ilex aquifolium* 'Silver Queen', for example, is, despite its name, a male plant, so will not bear red berries to detract from your garden's silvery theme.

Perfect Pastel Shades

Use the softest of pastel flowers to lighten your garden colour scheme. Tranquil pools of pink, blue and mauve help to add a sense of space.

S & O Mathews

Andrew Lawson

There is just as much design scope for the gardener in using pastel shades to create a border as there is with more intense colours (above). This border is dominated by two forms of **Lavatera;** *the tree mallow (***L. olbia 'Rosea'***), and the paler-flowered* **L. thuringiaca.** *Pastel designs work on a smaller scale too, such as this springtime combination of a pink tulip with pale blue forget-me-nots (inset).*

Rooms decorated in pastel shades are relaxing to live in. The colours are soothing to the eye and complement spots of more vibrant colour, throwing them forward and softening their aggressive tones.

In your garden pastel colours give the same softening effect, and can also create an illusion of depth and space, especially if planted at the end of a vista. Pale flowers cool down and soften intense, hot colours in a mixed border, and act as buffers between blocks of primary colour.

Garden designers use pastels to guide your eye to a particular point or feature they wish to emphasize. Gertrude Jekyll, a leading 19th century garden designer and author, used pastels as a bridge, to show that there was to be a change in colour intensity.

A garden that is a riot of colour does not make for relax-

ation. Hot and strong colour combinations are fun in certain situations, but need to be leavened with subtler, softer tones for long term enjoyment.

Use a pastel version of a darker, stronger colour as a counterpoint. Here the pastel will at the same time soften and, by contrast with its subtle tones, seem to strengthen

Pat Brindley

John Glover/Garden Picture Library

The well-named spring starflower (Ipheion uniflorum) has white forms, but the colour best suited to pastel schemes is the blue of varieties such as 'Caeruleum' (above).

Ornamental onions carry remarkable spherical flower heads on tall stems; those of Allium rosenbachianum (right) are pale pink; others in the genus are pale blue, white, yellow or purple.

the darker colour.

You could, of course, create a complete garden in soft, pastel shades; however, the overall effect is unlikely to be satisfactory. Gardens need focal points of stronger colour to give them life and movement. A completely pale garden will dissolve into a wishy-washy, rather lifeless scene.

Spring pastels

Bright yellow is the predominant colour of early spring, when its warmth is certainly welcome. There are, however many spring bulbs that bring just as warm a glow to the garden, but in softer colours.

Pink tulips such as 'Clara Butt' and 'Greenland' make up pretty pastel displays. Underplant them with the pale blue of forget-me-nots to make a pin-cushion of colour.

Spring starflower (*Ipheion uniflorum*) suits the front of a mixed border or a sunny position on a rockery. Its mass of lovely, powder blue, starry flowers give definition at the edge of a bed. It does best in a

PLANT LIST

Silver foliage plants

Helichrysum petiolare	Summer ground cover/in hanging baskets
Artemisia ludoviciana	Mid-border/needs staking
Senecio maritima	Edging plant in summer bedding scheme
Lamb's ears	Mid or front of border

Pastel shrubs

Tree mallow (*Lavatera*)	Wispy stems, floating flowers, back of border
Deutzia	Clusters of pink flowers, back of mixed border
Rhododendrons/Camellias/ Azaleas	In containers or shrub border. Need acid soil and shelter from early morning sun in winter.
Ceanothus	Powder blue flowers, grow as specimen
Russian sage (*Perovskia atriplicifolia*)	Lavender blue flowers, focal plant
Catmint (*Nepeta mussinii*)	Light blue flowers, edging or tumbling from walls

Annuals

Spider flower (*Cleome spinosa*)	Light and airy flowers, half-hardy
Hollyhocks	Spires of pastel flowers, grow against house or at back of border
Flowering sage (*Salvia horminum*)	Available in single colours or mixed pastels, use in middle of border

Pastel bulbs

Tulips	Plant in full sun
Lily of the valley	Naturalize in woodland setting, moist soils
Allium spp.	Plant at depth of three times height of individual bulbs
Nerine	Plant in full sun
Autumn crocus	Naturalize in semi-shade.

Edging plants

Pinks	Silver foliage and pink flowers, grow in sun in well-drained soil
Bugle (*Ajuga reptans*) 'Burgundy Glow'	Rosy foliage grows to make a good ground cover, suits rockery

Silver foliage is the perfect partner for pastel coloured flowers. To keep the soft pastel look going into late summer, grow *Sedum* 'Autumn Joy' next to lamb's ears (*Stachys lanata*). The flat flower heads of sedum turn from pale green at the bud stage to pale pink as they open. The silver foliage and soft, woolly textured flowers of lamb's ears offer contrasting shapes and textures and emphasize the softness of the pastels.

sheltered site in well-drained soil in sun or shade.

To lighten up a shady area, mix white and pink varieties of lily of the valley. The rosy ripple effect of the mixture in late spring will make a fragrant pool of delicate colour.

Summer bulbs

For dramatic shape, providing washes of pastel colour that seem to float in the border, use several different species of ornamental onions (*Allium* spp). The lilac flowered *A. giganteum* is a tall plant for the back of the border. The massive pin-cushion flower head of *A. albopilosum* (syn. *A. christophii*) is also lilac-coloured, though with a metallic sheen.

With heads of deeper mauve, bell-shaped flowers, *A. cernuum* is useful in the middle to front of a border, while

A. siculum, with its creamy and rosy pink flowers is perfect for the middle of the bed.

Plant ornamental onions in well-drained, sunny situations in autumn. Each onion should be planted at a depth of about three times the size of the individual bulb.

For autumn splendour, choose nerines such as *Nerine bowdenii* 'Pink Triumph'. Grow them in a sunny border at the edge of the patio or against the house.

Another useful plant at this time of year is the autumn crocus (*Colchicum autumnale*). The double-flowered form 'Roseum Plenum' makes a pretty splash of subtle colour when it is naturalized in a semi-shady woodland setting. Autumn crocus grows well in well-drained soil. It suits a woodland setting best, as its

rather floppy, strap-shaped spring leaves look untidy in a more formal planting.

Mixed borders

Bear's breeches (*Acanthus spinosus*) has an unusual and eye-catching spire of white flowers that deepen to mauve. Its deeply-cut, spiny leaves offer good complementary colour for a a pastel accent at the back of a wide border.

It enjoys full sun, but needs a well-drained, sandy soil. After flowering cut it back hard to ground level.

Japanese anemone (*Anemone* × *hybrida*, syn. *A. japon-*

ica) grows up to 1.2m/4ft. Its pastel pink flowers float on thin stems, offering delicate colour to bridge blues and deeper pinks in the border.

Delphinium Belladonna hybrids 'Pink Sensation' and 'Blue Bees' offer free flowering cup-shaped blooms on stems up to 1m/3ft long. They can be used to make blocks of soft cottage garden colour in the middle of a border.

The pale blue flowers of perennial flax (*Linum narbonense*) can be planted in deep

All deutzias flower profusely, most in shades of pink or white. D. longifolia 'Veitchii' (right) bears its five-petalled flowers in huge clusters.

Another abundant flowerer is the perennial flax (Linum narbonense). This offers a pastel colour scheme not only an abundance of small, blue summer flowers, but also a thicket of grey-green, lance-shaped leaves (below).

The California lilacs (Ceanothus spp.) are a large genus of small trees and shrubs, most with delightful pastel-blue flowers. C × veitchianus (right) is typical, bearing dense clusters of flowers from late spring into the summer. Given a sunny spot – and preferably a south or west-facing wall – this species will top 3m/10ft.

Photos Horiticultural

Eric Crichton

swathes through the border to highlight darker blues. It grows to 60cm/2ft. Though perennial, it is relatively short-lived. Renew it with plants raised from seed.

On the edge

Pastel colours, although pale, make good edging plants, drawing a soft line to enclose the border. Pastels tend to merge into clouds of colour, so the effect can often be quite loose and informal.

Modern pinks (*Dianthus allwoodii*) make a perfect pastel edge, producing successive flushes of flowers over several months in summer to provide a soft informality, while the neat silver mounds of their foliage make a more formal edging material.

On a rockery, varieties of bugle (*Ajuga reptans*), such as 'Burgundy Glow', make a soft and rosy mat that softens the rock contours. Foliage provides the pastel shades, complemented in summer with mauve or blue flowers.

A large palette

Large shrubs offer much for the pastel garden. Tree mallow (*Lavatera olbia* 'Rosea') carries its soft pink hollyhock-like flowers on wispy stems that spread through other plants in a mixed shrub border. It suits the back of a sunny, well-drained border and can reach up to 3m/10ft.

In early summer, deutzia (*Deutzia longifolia* 'Veitchii') offers large clusters of small, soft pink flowers carried on elegant arching stems. It looks attractive as a specimen shrub or mixed into a shrub and perennial border.

Acid lovers

Rhododendrons, azaleas and camellias, too, are available in a wide range of soft pastel pinks and creamy pinks. They all need an acid soil with good drainage as well as partial shade and shelter from early morning winter sun.

Dwarf forms of rhododendron and most camellias and azaleas are suited to container growing. On a balcony or patio they provide evergreen foliage and spring flowers.

For a wealth of pastel blue flowers grow the California lilac (*Ceanothus* 'Autumnal Blue'). It flowers freely from late spring through to autumn, with long panicles of tiny, powder blue flowers, and eventually reaches a height and spread of 3m/10ft. It can be grown against or near a house wall, providing you give it support and tie it in.

Russian sage (*Perovskia atriplicifolia*), a low-growing shrub (up to 1m/3ft), and cat-

Peter McHoy

mint (*Nepeta mussinii*) provide lavender-coloured flowers in great profusion. Both look attractive in mixed borders. Catmint is often used as an edging plant and thrives on well-drained, light soils.

Annual events

Hollyhocks provide pastel pinks and creamy whites that will soften and romanticize your mixed border. Grow them in a bed against the house to take advantage of their cottage garden look.

Ageratum, alyssum and candytuft are low-growing, and their pastel colours make them suitable for the front of the summer bedding scheme.

For the back of the bed try the spider flower (*Cleome spinosa*), which has a rose to mauve colour range. Half-hardy, it is easily grown from seed and can be planted out in early summer in well-drained soil in full sun.

Varieties of cosmos (*Cosmea bipinnatus*), including 'Daydream', 'Sensation Mixed' and 'Sea Shells', have large daisy-shaped flowers in soft colours. Popular annuals, including love-in-a-mist, pansy and busy Lizzie, are also available in pale shades that will work well in summer bedding or in mixed containers.

Sage advice

Flowering sage (*Salvia horminum*), particularly the varieties 'Pink Sage' and 'Mixed Art

The unusually-shaped blooms of the spider flower (Cleome spinosa syn. C. hassleriana) are white flushed with pink in the species, but cultivated varieties produce a wide palette of pretty pastels. Perhaps the most colourful is the aptly-named 'Colour Fountain' (top), with flowers in shades of pink, mauve and purple. The annual ageratums have a similar colour range (above), but include several lovely blue varieties.

Catmint (Nepeta x fassennii), a bushy perennial which is frequently planted near paths or in borders, produces a mass of pretty, lavender-blue flowers (facing page) in early summer.

Shades', is the perfect pastel bridge in your colour scheme. Use the single colour form as a solid block as you move towards more intense colours. The mixed shades will be useful to cool down a collection of warmer colours. Pastel forms of flowering sage do best in partial shade.

ROSY TINTS

Old garden roses offer a wide range of lovely full-blown shapes and delicate pastel shades. *Rosa* 'Maiden's Blush' has fragrant, double, pinky-white summer flowers. Rosa mundi (*Rosa gallica* 'Versicolor') offers wider, flatter flowers with crimson streaks on a pink-washed background.

Old garden roses have a lax form that suits an informal cottage-garden border.

DON'T FORGET!

BRIGHT IDEAS

TWILIGHT BED

In strong sun, pastel coloured flowers may look washed out and even paler than they are. But at night, when light is dimmer, the paler colours become more reflective and seem to glow. For this reason plant a pastel bed near the house, so that you can enjoy its night-time shimmering.

Improving Soil with Compost

Few soils are perfect and when moving to a new home the garden you inherit is a matter of pot-luck. There are, however, ways to improve soils.

The easiest way to judge a soil's composition is to pick up a handful and to rub a sample between your thumb and first finger. If it creates a smooth, slippery, greasy surface, the sample contains clay. If rough and gritty, it is predominantly sand.

Another test is to slightly moisten some soil and roll it into a sausage, then curl this to form a ring. The smaller the ring – without breaking – the higher the clay content.

A further test is to fill a screw-top jar about a quarter full with soil, first removing any large stones. Fill the jar three-quarters full with cold

Eric Crichton

A quick-growing crop such as mustard (left) can be dug into a bed to 'green manure' it. Plants grown next year will benefit.

Add compost to the bottom of the trench (top right) when double digging.

Waterlogged ground must be drained (bottom right) unless you want a boggy area.

Spread compost over the soil and fork it in (below) before sowing or planting.

Collections/Patrick Johns

GROWING TIPS

GREEN MANURING

This involves growing quick-maturing crops, such as annual lupins, mustard, Italian rye, Hungarian rye or red clover, and digging them into the soil before they flower and produce seeds. This introduces organic material into the soil and increases its fertility.

Green manuring is best reserved for vegetable plots, or perhaps large flower beds that are being replanned and will not be replanted for a year.

water, screw on the lid and shake the jar vigorously for several minutes.

The mixture settles in layers – stones at the base, followed by coarse and light sand, then silt and clay. Organic material floats on the surface. The proportions will indicate the soil's nature.

Although not scientific, the 'boot' test usually says all one needs to know about clay soils. If, after walking over the soil – especially in winter – it sticks to your boots, you can be sure it is mainly clay.

Taming the extremes

The dream garden has soil that is a balance between clay and sand – friable and light to

LIVING IMPROVERS

Soil organisms such as fungi, algae, protozoa and bacteria are microscopic. They are vital for breaking down compounds in the soil for subsequent use by plants. Without these hidden warriors the soil would become dead and unable to grow plants.

Garden worms are frequently detested because they create worm casts on lawns. They are, however, valuable soil improvers, aerating and mixing the soil by their activities.

GO ORGANIC!

should apply depends on the soil's acidity (see box).

You can help improve small areas by adding coarse sand or fine gravel. These physically open up the soil, improving drainage and aeration. However, to make a significant improvement you must add at least one or two buckets per square metre/square yard.

Shredded bark also opens up soil, but other than for the improvement of small areas its cost prohibits extensive use.

Putting in drains is essential if water remains on the surface in winter. It is pointless improving surface areas in clay soils if the underlying water is not drained. Modern slit drains are much less effort to install than traditional tile or rubble land drains.

Sandy soils need copious amounts of bulky organic material, such as farmyard manure and garden compost. Peat is ideal if the soil is alkaline, while spent mushroom compost is best if the area is acid.

Spent hops are ideal for improving sandy soils, but are difficult to obtain.

Because sandy soil is exceptionally well aerated, bulky organic materials soon decay. Therefore, be prepared to dig in these materials every year, as well as applying mulches in spring or early summer.

It is not without good reason that an old gardening adage says that sandy soils need a thunderstorm every month and a load of manure every other month!

Apply general balanced fertilizers every spring and install a hose sprinkler system for important areas such as vegetable plots, summer flower beds and lawns.

Silts are best treated in the same way as clay soils, as they tend to have an acid nature.

DOUBLE DIGGING

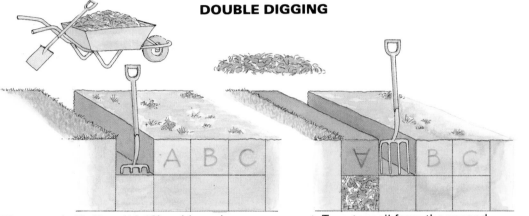

Dig a trench 30-45cm/12-18in wide and one spade's depth. Put the soil in a barrow. Fork over the bottom of the trench and add compost. Turn topsoil from the second trench into the first. Continue and fill the last trench with soil from the barrow.

Michael Shoebridge

Peter McHoy

handle, yet moisture-retentive and well aerated.

Gardening, however, can be a perverse hobby. Although neighbouring gardens may have a perfect loam, yours will be formed totally of heavy clay or entirely of sand. There are, however, ways to improve both of these extremes.

Clay soils are improved by digging in, during winter, as much bulky organic material as possible, especially farmyard and stable manure, garden compost, peat and spent mushroom compost.

Calcium compounds dusted over the surface are also beneficial. They encourage clay particles to form small groups and this improves drainage and aeration. The amount you

A to Z of improving soil

● **Bracken** when chopped up makes a good mulch, but beware of its sharp stems which can cut your hands.

TYPES OF COMPOST

The term 'compost' has several meanings and is often used confusingly.

- **Potting composts** are either loam-based or peat-based. The loam-based type is a mixture of loam, peat, sharp sand and fertilizers. Peat-based (loam-less) composts are mainly formed of peat. Peat substitute composts are now available. Plants are transferred into these composts when too large for their previous containers, whether a seed-tray where they were sown, or a small pot.
- **Seed composts** are similar to potting composts, but they are formulated for the sowing of seeds.
- **Garden compost** is decayed vegetative material, created in a compost heap from kitchen waste and garden plants. It is either dug into the soil or used to create a mulch on the soil's surface. Details of how to make a compost heap were in part 2.

Dry, sandy soils will absorb and benefit from large amounts of organic material such as garden compost (left). It will improve their fertility and their ability to hold water.

If you can get large amounts of well-rotted farmyard manure (above right) it can be used in many parts of the garden. Here, it has been heaped on an artichoke trench. Riding stables are a good source of horse manure.

A mulch (right) will keep the soil moist and will also feed it as the organic material gradually decomposes.

Collections/Patrick Johns

Marshall Cavendish

ALKALINE OR ACID?

Clay soils can be improved by dusting the surface with lime, which makes soil particles clump together, but first it is essential to know how acid the soil is. The higher the soil acidity, the more lime can be used. Incidentally, sandy soils can also be acid, although it is usually peaty soils that are acid.

Judging the soil's pH (acidity or alkalinity) is easy. There are proprietary kits where a sample of soil is mixed with water then matched with a colour-coded strip that indicates the pH. More expensive are testers with probes that are inserted into the soil. The pH is indicated on a dial.

The cheapest test is with a piece of chemically-treated card. This is inserted into a soil and water mixture, and the resulting colour is compared with a colour code that indicates the pH.

- **Digging** ground in winter is the traditional way to aerate soil, improve drainage, incorporate bulky organic materials and to bury annual weeds. Also, many soil pests become exposed to winter weather and birds, and this helps to reduce their numbers.
- **Farmyard manure** is a legendary soil improver. Never use fresh manure, as during its subsequent breakdown in the soil it absorbs nitrogen, causing temporary starvation around plants. Also, roots and stems are scorched by fresh manure. Use well-rotted manure, digging it into the ground during winter.

After delivery, keep manure covered until it is dug in – rain leaches nutrients from it.

Do not apply manure and lime at the same time, as the nitrogen will be lost into the atmosphere in the form of ammonia. If manure is dug into the soil in early winter, wait until mid-winter before applying a dusting of lime.

- **Garden compost** is formed from soft-tissued, pest- and disease-free plants that have been encouraged to decay until they become crumbly. This usually takes about six months; decomposition speeds

Eric Crichton

Marshall Cavendish

Autumn leaves (above) will break down into rich leaf mould, as on this fork. Leaves must be composted, either on their own if you have enough of them, or you can add them to your compost heap.

MAKING YOUR SOIL LESS ACID	Soil	Hydrated lime	Ground limestone
The amount of lime needed to counteract acidity depends on the pH of the soil, the type of soil and the form in which the lime is applied.	Clay	425g/sq m (18oz/sq yd)	575g/sq m (24oz/sq yd)
	Loam	285g/sq m (12oz/sq yd)	380g/sq m (16oz/sq yd)
As a guide, the following amounts of lime will reduce acidity by about 1.0 pH.	Sand	140g/sq m (6oz/sq yd)	190g/sq m (8oz/sq yd)

Remember:

- Apply only sufficient lime to bring the pH to 6.5.
- The pH figure should only be taken as a guide. On dry soils (especially when assessed by a probe) the reading may indicate that the soil is more acid than it really is. Conversely, readings taken in late winter can indicate too high alkalinity.
- Avoid excessive liming as it leads to deficiencies of iron and manganese.
- Apply lime after digging the soil in early winter, dusting it over the surface so that subsequently rain will wash it into the ground; surface lime damages plants.

up in wet, warm summers.

Compost can be dug into the soil in winter or used to form a mulch on the surface during spring and early summer.

Do not compost thick, woody stems, perennial weeds or plants that have been treated with weedkillers.

- **Hay** forms a mulch, as well as keeping strawberry fruits off the ground and preventing them from being damaged by rain splashing off the soil during torrential storms.
- **Hoeing** is a routine job, creating a tilth on the surface of the soil, reducing water loss and removing weeds.
- **Leafmould** is created from decayed leaves and is used as a mulch or for digging into the soil in winter.
- **Mulching** is an excellent way to prevent the growth of weeds. It keeps the soil cool during summer, feeds it and assists in moisture retention.

Mulches are applied in late spring and early summer, as soon as the soil has warmed up. Water the soil well first.

Mulches of 7.5-10cm/3-4in are best, using well-rotted manure, compost, peat, shredded bark, chopped bracken, sawdust, straw, hay or leafmould.

Newspapers and corrugated cardboard can also be used, but need topping with something like pulverized bark to improve the appearance and prevent them blowing about.

Plastic sheeting is used, but this does not rot down and improve the soil's texture.

- **Peat** has long been used as a mulch and is often added to the soil when planting. However, it is a limited natural resource and its continuing use destroys many acres of peat beds each year.
- **Sand and fine gravel** open up clay soils, but need to be applied generously.
- **Sawdust** is a useful mulch, especially around gooseberries and currant bushes.
- **Seaweed** contains potash and trace elements and is superb for digging into sandy soils in early winter, as it is slow to rot. Do not use it in large amounts as a mulch.

Potatoes and tomatoes grow especially well on land where seaweed has been dug in.

Unfortunately, it may be contaminated with oil and, on the west coast of Britain, is said to be slightly radioactive. Unless you live in a coastal area its transportation is prohibitively expensive.

- **Shredded bark** forms an attractive mulch. Garden shredders can be used to turn stiff-stemmed garden waste into a mulch material.
- **Spent mushroom compost,** which contains lime, is ideal for digging into acid soil.
- **Spent hops** are ideal for digging into sandy soils, and for creating a good mulch. Unfortunately, they are difficult to obtain.
- **Straw** is useful as a mulch around soft fruits, though it does encourage slugs.

73

Home-made Composts

Improve your soil while reducing waste by making your own garden compost. It is easy to do and very satisfying.

Making your own compost is perhaps the ultimate in recycling. There is nothing magical about composting: all plant and animal material will rot down eventually. By making a compost heap, you are just speeding up the process, concentrating it in one place.

In the past, garden compost was used both to enrich the soil and for growing seedlings and pot plants. There is now no point in using it as a growing medium as the widely available specialist composts produce much better results.

The nutrient value of your compost will depend on what has gone into it, but the main function of all garden compost is to contribute to the creation and maintenance of a healthy soil by nourishing the micro-organisms that live within it. These micro-organisms in turn release nutrients that will benefit your growing plants.

Better texture
Like all bulky organic material, including farmyard manure, compost helps free-draining sandy soils to retain moisture and conversely opens up sticky clay soils and helps them drain. Used regularly and fairly generously, this organic material helps to make the soil more workable and more able to support a wide range of plants.

Do not, however, expect instant results: feeding the soil is a slow, steady process and it takes time to see the benefits of continually adding compost.

Some experts manage to make compost-making sound very complicated. It need not be so. Garden compost is simply free organic matter and need not take hours of your

A cube- or cylinder-shaped bin is best as the contents will then heat up well and kill weeds and diseases. Your bin should be at least 1m³/3ft³.

Make sure you can get easy access to your compost: a cube-shaped bin should have a removable side; lids should be easy to lift on and off.

Cover your heap to keep heat in and rain out.

Marshall Cavendish

Keep a bucket in the kitchen and empty your vegetable waste into it instead of just throwing it out. You can use anything from egg shells to cabbage leaves, apple cores to leftover carrots – it will all make excellent compost. Once you have filled the bucket (left) tip the contents onto the compost heap where it will soon decompose. Do not mix it. Remove compost from the bottom of the heap at regular intervals.

A good compost heap should not be completely air-tight. Turning your heap will help to introduce air.

— A compost bin does not have to be made of wood: any good insulant will do.

— Site on soil so that worms, fungi and bacteria have access and can speed up decomposition.

produce your own food, especially organically, you will need to feed your garden a lot and will probably want to make as much compost as possible. Use everything you can, from the garden, the house and even what you can beg from the neighbours.

You can almost never overdo the amount of compost you add to the vegetable patch, especially where you intend to grow potatoes, peas, beans and other vegetables which need a lot of moisture in order to crop satisfactorily. Aim to dig in a full barrow-load for every square metre.

Using grass cuttings

If your garden is mainly ornamental, on the other hand, and you have a large lawn, the compost heap is a convenient way of dealing with all those mowings. Mowings on their own do not make a satisfactory compost — much more than 30 per cent of mowings will result in a slimy although still usable mess, and you will need other ingredients.

All the waste products from flower beds and borders will help, together with the various types of kitchen waste.

The compost you make can

be used as a mulch on the borders, around individual plants, or dug into the soil when you are preparing the ground for planting or are lifting, dividing or moving plants.

A mulch of compost

If you decide to use your compost as a mulch — a layer of material laid on bare soil to suppress weeds and retain moisture — you will need a 5-8cm/2-3in deep layer for it to be effective. When you apply the mulch, first place it around precious plants which could suffer during droughts and hosepipe bans. If you have any left over, spread it around other plants next, and finally on any bare ground. Be careful not to let the mulch touch the stems or trunks of any plants, as it could kill them — these parts are meant to be above

SPEED UP DECAY

Bag up weeds and accumulate kitchen waste until you next mow the lawn. Then add all these materials at the same time, so that the heat from the grass mowings can start work on the rest straight away.

SHORT CUTS

time to produce. Likewise, choosing what to add to your heap is not difficult. Suitable composting materials are anything that once lived, so do not restrict yourself to garden waste. Think about what you throw in the dustbin now: tea leaves, egg shells, vegetable peelings, for example.

How much to make

You do not need to make vast amounts of compost for it to be worthwhile. If you are keen to

Compost is a wonderful substance that can be used in a number of ways. In autumn it can be used as a feed. It will not only add valuable nutrients but it will also greatly improve the soil texture. It should be dug into the soil with a spade. This is especially useful for any vegetables you may be growing. Alternatively it can be used at any other time of the year as a mulch (right) or be forked into the soil around shrubs.

Andrew Lawson

Marshall Cavendish

Compost bins can be bought in a wide variety of forms and work in slightly different ways, but the end product is invariably very similar. This wire mesh bin (left) is fairly inconspicuous and allows lots of air to circulate, ensuring rapid breakdown of the compostable material. For something that looks a bit more professional this twin bin (below) is made from strong steel tubes and rot proof material which allows the air to circulate. Fill the first bin and allow the compost to make while you fill up the second. The compost which is ready is easily removed from the base.

WHAT TO ADD TO A COMPOST HEAP

- plant material
- lawn mowings
- wood ash
- kitchen waste, including vegetable parings and tea bags
- newspaper and other waste paper
- sawdust and straw
- finger-thick woody prunings
- thorny prunings (wear gloves when handling compost – thorns stay intact)
- manure mixed with 'bedding' (for example, straw, shredded paper or sawdust)
- droppings from poultry, pigeons and farm animals

MAKING A COMPOST HEAP

You can use wood, mesh panels, a plastic dustbin or barrel or even straw bales. Make sure you incorporate enough ventilation when you are building, or drill holes in solid sides. If you use mesh, line your bin with cardboard or plastic sheeting to reduce some of the airflow. Make sure you can get easy access to the heap, for adding and removing material.

The first layer of the heap should be brushwood, thick woody prunings or tough stems (e.g. cabbage). Lay this directly on the soil to help ventilation.

Add your compostable material in 15-30cm/6-12in layers. Each layer should be a well-mixed combination of soft, sappy greenery (like mowings) and drier, coarser material (like dead flower stalks or woody prunings). Water this layer if necessary to make it moist but not sodden and fit the lid.

Start collecting material again until you have enough to add another layer and repeat the process. Once the container is full, leave it with the lid on until the contents have rotted and you need to use it. Keep the outer edges for adding to the new heap as they will not have rotted down completely.

ground, not buried!

There are three main options when choosing where to make compost: burying compostable material in a trench; placing it in a bought or home-made container; or simply building a heap.

Making a trench

Burying compostable material in a trench is an ideal method for use with bare ground where you intend to grow vegetables. It gets rid of the need for a heap or bin and once you have dug your trench, all you have to do is place mowings

WHAT WENT WRONG?

Q Last year I decided to make my own compost from lawn-mowings, but after 12 months all I have got is a slimy mess that smells frankly offensive.

A This happens when too many grass mowings are added, all at once. Your 'compost' can still be used – dig it into the ground or spread it as a mulch – but in future, mix dry and bulky material with the mowings and you will get better results.

This compost is unsuitable for use, in parts it has not decayed and in others it is too slimy.

Q The ingredients of my compost look just the same now as they did six months ago. Why should this be and what can I do?

A Your heap has not become hot enough to start decomposition. Re-build it, including a source of nitrogen – mowings, nettles, comfrey or urine – to help the bacteria to digest the heap. Prevent drying out by lining a bin with cardboard or cover a heap with polythene.

WHAT NOT TO ADD TO A COMPOST HEAP

- diseased plant material
- coal ash
- bones
- meat scraps (as these attract vermin)
- cardboard
- lumps of soil
- very thick prunings (unless shredded first)
- seeding weeds and roots of perennial weeds (unless the heap is very hot)
- dog and cat manure (unless the heap is very hot and compost is not to be used on food crops)
- tree leaves (make a separate leaf heap)

Eric Crichton

and other material into the base. When you have a fairly thick layer, cover it with soil and tread it down.

Waste composted in this way will not heat up much, so you will not be able to put perennial weeds and seedheads in the trench and you will also have to avoid adding anything which animals may want to dig up. Leave it to rot until the following spring, then plant your vegetables – especially moisture-loving runner beans – or potato tubers.

If you do not have enough bare ground to bury your

If you don't want to go out and buy a compost bin why not build your own? It doesn't have to be anything too complicated but a cube or cylindrical shape is best. This bin (above right) has been made from wood and the mesh front ensures there is plenty of ventilation. Easy access to the heap is important. This bin allows you to add material to the top and to slide the mesh panel up to enable you to remove compost from the bottom.

waste, you will need a compost heap or bin. Your bin need not be large as mowings and other material sink down surprisingly quickly. Start with a small container and buy or make a second one if the first begins to overflow.

Natural allies

Whichever type you choose, place it directly on to the soil so that the fungi, bacteria and worms, which all contribute to the decomposition process, have access to it.

The commonest bins on sale are either plastic cylinder shapes or cubes made of wood slats or mesh panels. Slats and mesh can let in too much air, so you may have to line the sides with plastic to cut down on draughts. Neither type is very expensive, but you could easily make your own.

The right mixture

Provided you put in a good mixture of materials, ensure the right amount of air and keep the heap damp, you should be able to make good compost in any container.

If you think of a compost heap as similar in principle to a fire, you will appreciate what is needed. Fuel, in the form of compostable material: air, to

fan the flames but not put them out; and heat, which in turn helps more heat be generated, are all essential.

With a small compost heap, after the initial heat has diminished, mix up or 'turn' the contents, so that the material that was formerly on the outside is on the inside. This process adds more air to the remaining uncomposted material and re-kindles the 'fire'. To avoid doing this manually, you can buy tumbler bins which you regularly turn on their axis to re-mix the contents, but this can be hard work as the bin gets fuller.

GREEN FEED

A compost heap is the basis of good organic gardening and is also a productive way of re-cycling various materials. Do not limit yourself to re-cycling your garden waste; save your kitchen waste too (in a covered bucket). Use natural or recycled materials to construct your bin and mowings, nettles, comfrey or urine as a nitrogen source to speed decay. For true organic gardening use ingredients from organic gardens and farms only.

...nfrey leaves or stinging nettles on ...mpost heap will add nutrients and ...ed up decay.

Using Fertilizers

Keeping your soil nourished with the right feed is vital for healthy, attractive plants. Find out what kind of soil you have, and what fertilizer it needs most.

A dressing of organic bone meal on a freshly dug vegetable plot in autumn. It needs to be forked in to the soil.

Fertilizers will help to make your garden soil more fertile and productive. They improve sandy and peaty soils which are not very fertile. They also replace nutrients where constant cropping has robbed the soil of the plant waste that would otherwise have been returned to the ground to rot down (thus recycling the nutrients).

Using fertilizers is just as important in your fruit and vegetable garden, where you remove all or part of a plant, as it is on farmland.

Modern methods

When you prune or harvest a plant, you are removing some of its food reserves, and these have to be replaced. Fertilizers are also useful on your lawn, if you always remove the dead grass clippings.

Fertilizers were originally applied in the form of animal dung, garden compost, seaweed or crushed, quarried minerals that were rich in certain nutrients.

WHICH FERTILIZER?

Fertilizer	Uses	Source	Features
Nitrogen (N)	When the whole plant appears weak and the lower, older leaves are yellow, small and curling, and the plant flowers and fruits poorly.	Urea Blood Hoof and horn Soot (old) Seaweed Ammonium sulphate Nitrates (various)	Organic, fast, acidic Organic, fast, acidic Organic, fast, acidic Organic, fast, neutral Organic, steady, neutral Inorganic, fast, acidic Inorganic, fast, most neutral
Phosphorus (P)	If older leaves have red or purple margins, and are small, drop prematurely and the plant is dark green and stunted.	Bone meal Seaweed Basic slag Mineral phosphate Super-phosphate	Organic, slow, alkaline Organic, steady, neutral Inorganic, slow, alkaline Inorganic, steady, alkaline Inorganic, steady, neutral
Potassium (K)	When older leaf margins are scorched and there are small spots of dead tissue at the leaf tip and between the veins	Wood ashes *Potassium sulphate *Potassium nitrate	Organic, fast, alkaline Inorganic, steady, acidic Inorganic, fast, alkaline

*Potassium sulphate is also known as sulphate of potash
*Potassium nitrate is also known as nitrate of potash

Dried Blood
Organic nitrogen fertiliser for rapid plant growth

Hoof and horn

Bone meal

Wood ashes

Blood

Ammonium sulphate

Seaweed extract

Nitrogen (N)

Phosphorus (P)

Potassiu

Nowadays most fertilizers used in agriculture and horticulture are manufactured synthetically. These are known as inorganic fertilizers, because they are not produced from once-living matter.

Restoring soil

Plants and flowers require many chemicals in small amounts for healthy growth. Some, especially nitrogen, which is required for leaf growth, are absorbed from the soil in greater quantities than others, quickly exhausting the supply.

Those elements required in the greatest quantity – nitrogen, potassium and phosphorus – are known as major nutrients. Other chemicals in the soil, known as minor nutrients, are also necessary to plants but are used in such

After aerating the lawn in autumn apply a sedge peat dressing and brush it into the holes to improve the soil (right). Then apply an autumn lawn fertilizer that is low in nitrogen and high in phosphorus to encourage root growth.

Pat Brindley

Fertilizer	Uses	Source	Features
Calcium (Ca)	If newer leaves and tips of shoots are turned inward, ragged, scorched or even dead. But first look for caterpillars and aphids, which cause curling on leaves	Calcium compounds Lime/chalk Gypsum	Inorganic, fast, alkaline Organic, slow, alkaline Inorganic, slow, acidic
Magnesium (Mg)	When older leaves are mottled with spots of dead tissue and the leaf margins curl upwards and have slender stalks. But these symptoms may also be the result of excessive potassium fertilizer.	Kieserite/ dolomitic limestone Epsom salts/ magnesium sulphate	Organic, slow, alkaline Inorganic, steady, alkaline
Iron (Fe)	If newer leaves are yellow or bleached, with the veins remaining green, and the plant is growing poorly.	Iron sulphate Sequestrene	Inorganic, steady, acidic Inorganic, steady, neutral Cures iron deficiency.

small quantities that there is rarely a deficiency of them.

Plants in containers can also exhaust the soil's nutrients, major and minor, and need to be fed with fertilizers for good growth.

If you do not use fertilizer the plants will grow less well and be far more likely to succumb to pests and diseases. The exceptions are some culinary herbs, which thrive on poor soils, and should not be fed with fertilizers.

Choice of food

Whatever soil and type of garden you have, you need to supply a balanced diet to your plants. Bulky fertilizers such as stable or farmyard manure mixed with straw should contain a little of everything, and will improve the drainage of sticky soils, while helping dry soils to retain moisture for longer than usual. Manures should be stacked for a few months before they are used.

Many people, especially those living in towns, have no access to manure and use peat instead. But peat does not contain any nutrients.

For town dwellers, the main alternative to manure is garden compost. This can provide the whole range of nutrients in the same way that manure and straw do.

Lawn mowings make a good base for composting and, when mixed with shredded paper and kitchen waste, should allow you to produce enough compost for the vegetable garden and also some to place in

3kg

Lime/chalk

Magnesium sulphate

Epsom salts

Sequestrene

Calcium (Ca)   Magnesium (Mg)   Iron (Fe)

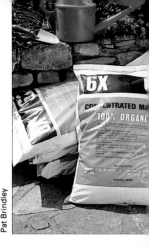

TESTING THE SOIL

- A simple test kit will show if your soil lacks vital nutrients, and will tell you whether the soil is acid or alkaline.
- Test the soil in spring and you will know what to expect in the coming season. You will also learn what the soil is lacking and, therefore, what you must add.
- Foliage plants such as lettuce and grass may need plenty of nitrogen. A plant grown for its flowers or fruits could need more potassium. Root growth is stimulated by phosphorus.
- General fertilizers benefit all plants. Apply a single element fertilizer only if the soil is low in one nutrient.

---

planting holes for ornamental plants. If you have no space for a compost heap you can buy bagged up manure-based composts.

Bulky manures supply the complete range of nutrients, albeit in very small amounts. But some plants need more of some elements than manure or garden compost can provide. You will have to add these extra elements in the form of concentrates.

Strike a balance between your use of fertilizers and farmyard manure or garden compost. Use manure or compost for the value of their physical bulk and use fertilizers to feed your plants.

Organic gardens

It is important to give plants the exact nutrients they need. So consider whether or not you want to use organic methods.

Organic growing is based on the long-term health of the soil. It uses bulky manures and nutrients that feed the soil organisms as well as the plants. These nutrients are supplied by organic fertilizers, which means that they have

been produced from once-living matter, such as bone meal or compost.

Limestone, formed from the shells of ancient sea creatures, is an organic fertilizer, and quarried rock phosphate and potash (potassium) are also used by organic growers.

Organic fertilizers usually have to be broken down by organisms in the soil before their chemicals take a form which can be used by the plant. So, usually, they have a steady or slow effect on the plants, though this is not always the case. The exceptions are blood, urea and wood ashes.

Fast action

Inorganic fertilizers provide the same chemicals to the plants but in a soluble form with a fast effect. Their solubility means that some of these manufactured fertilizers can be quickly washed away from the root zone.

To counter this, firms have developed controlled, or slow-release, fertilizers for lawns, flower beds and pot plants. The particles of fertilizer are bound with a substance which either allows the nutrients to pass through gradually when wetted, or needs bacterial action to break down the coating. These coated particles are those often mistaken for slugs' eggs in the potting compost of purchased plants.

Choosing with care

Fertilizers are sold as straights, compounds and soil improvers. Straights are those which contain one nutrient, such as superphosphate, which provides phosphorus, or ammonium sulphate (sulphate of ammonia), which provides nitrogen.

Compounds are a mixture of materials which give a variety of nutrients in a certain ratio. You will find this ratio printed on the package.

The items are always listed in the order of nitrogen, phosphorus and potassium (often re-

ferred to as N:P:K, the abbreviations used by chemists), followed by other components.

For example, when you see a ratio described as 7:7:7, this shows an equal amount of nitrogen, phosphorus and potassium. The figures 10:0:6 would indicate that no phosphorus is contained in this particular compound.

The actual figures used refer to the percentage of each nutrient. So 7:7:7 shows that each component forms seven per cent of the compound.

You also find that the package shows the proportions of other nutrients in the overall weight of the compound. So 10g/kg means that 10 grammes of the nutrient is present in every kilogramme, or 1000 grammes, of the fertilizer, which works out at one per cent. This is handy to know when comparing brands.

Special treatment

Fertilizers are often sold for specialist uses. These include tomato fertilizer, chrysanthemum feed and spring or summer lawn dressing. If you look at the ratio given on the package, you will see that many are similar.

Tomato fertilizer, for example, which is only used once the fruit sets, contains a high proportion of potash which is required by the developing

Those without access to farmyard manure and without space for a compost heap can buy bags of concentrated organic manure (top). Though not cheap, it is convenient. Fertilizers are best applied to seed beds before planting (above).

Foliar feeds (above) are sprayed onto a plant's leaves. Here one is being applied to perk up a weak rhododendron. Add lime (below) to a lawn if a soil test shows the soil to be very acid. This is a rare problem as most grasses tolerate acidity.

tered over the surface of the soil and raked in before sowing or planting. This process is called base dressing. When applied to growing plants, it is known as top dressing.

Handling and storage

Dry fertilizer has to be weighed out for accurate dosing and can blow into your eyes during use on all but the stillest day. Lawn fertilizer spreaders are sold which help you to apply the material evenly. Take care not to overlap or miss strips as you apply it, or you will have stripes of different greens on the lawn.

These dry fertilizers must be stored in a dry place. If they get wet they will set rock hard in their packs and be extremely difficult to use. The packs are easily damaged and can leak the material everywhere. Fertilizer is also very corrosive to metals so keep it well away from your car.

Special dry mix fertilizers can be bought to add to other ingredients, such as loam, peat, perlite and sand, to make your own potting compost.

Keeping stocks

Some dry fertilizers can be diluted with water and kept as concentrated stock solution, to be diluted further when required. You can also buy liquid fertilizers that are ready to dilute; these can be kept in a damp place.

Liquid feeds can often be applied to leaves, and not just the soil, and can be used in a hose-end dilutor to spray the material to the far corners of flower borders and beds.

Hose-end dilutors also make feeding the lawn easy, with no danger of leaving stripes, and save you carrying watering cans across the garden. Some hose-end dilutors are designed to take tablet fertilizers.

Correct timing

It is important to apply fertilizer at the correct time. The fast-acting types will soon be

fruits. It can be used for most flowering plants if necessary. Foliage plants, however, prefer fertilizers high in nitrogen.

Liquid or dry

Fertilizers can be applied as liquids or as dry granules or powders. Dry fertilizer is scat-

---

GARDEN NOTES

FEEDING PLANTS

● The way your plants grow tells you what nutrients are lacking and need replacement.
● Some plants take up a nutrient early in the growing season and quickly exhaust the supply.
● Look out for signs of deficiency in the growing season, not in autumn when the leaves change colour and die.
● General purpose fertilizers supply a balance of the major nutrients. For specific nutrients, choose one that is readily available to you.

SOILS THAT 'LOCK UP' FERTILIZERS

Some plants find it difficult to absorb certain nutrients – particularly iron – from neutral or acid soils. Acid-loving plants, in particular, such as rhododendrons, camellias, skimmias and most heathers, find that the nutrients are 'locked up' chemically.

Using fertilizers that make the soil more acid (sulphate of ammonia instead of Nitro-chalk if you want a nitrogenous fertilizer, for example) may help over time, but can never be an adequate solution on a very chalky soil.

For more immediate results you can use a product called Sequestrene, which provides the necessary nutrients in a form that acid-loving plants can absorb even on ordinary soils.

Sequestrene is available as a powder or granules, so it can be diluted and watered on the soil or added dry and left for the rain to wash in.

---

washed from the soil, beyond the reach of the plants, so apply them at the appropriate stage of growth, which is usually the spring.

Slow-acting types can be effective for a year or more, so the timing is less critical, especially if you apply them annually or more often to ensure a continual supply to your valuable plants.

It is better to apply dry material to growing plants with dry leaves. If the leaves are wet from dew or rain, the material can stick to the leaves and scorch them.

If you are foliar feeding, do so on a dry day so that the nutrients stay on the leaves where the plants can quickly take them up. If washed off onto the soil, the effect may be slower.

Nitrogen encourages soft, leafy growth, so avoid applying it after mid-summer, or new growths could be damaged by the first frosts and cold winds.

Controlling Pests

Gardeners often worry about pests and the damage that they may cause. However, prompt action of the right sort will usually prevent them becoming a problem.

Not all creatures are pests and many of those labelled as pests are unlikely to be a major problem in your garden. But it pays to be familiar with the common pests and the problems they cause.

Gardeners have come to rely on remedies out of a pesticide bottle, but often there is a cheaper and simpler way of dealing with the problem. A combination of good gardening practice, eagle eyes and resorting to chemicals only when necessary, should keep pest numbers below problem levels.

Organic controls (which will be looked at in more detail in a later issue) avoid the use of any chemical except those derived from plants. But unfortunately these pesticides are often non-selective, killing all in their path, including pest predators. Modern specific pesticides are more useful.

Problem areas

Pests can build up in gardens because there are many similar plants growing together. These provide a good meal and breeding sites for creatures that then become pests, damaging the appearance and yield of your plants.

If you have little time free for gardening, it makes sense to choose plants that are not troubled by pests. Avoid, for instance, roses, which can become smothered in greenfly and sooty mould to the extent that their blooms are spoiled.

In a greenhouse or conservatory, the sheltered environment and abundance of food enable pest numbers to build

Andrew Lawson

Peter McHoy

Don Wildridge

Weevils (above) cut scalloped holes from the edges of leaves.

Sawfly larvae (left) can cause extensive damage to leaves.

When spraying (opposite page), wear protective gloves and make sure to spray the underside of leaves where pests often hide.

up. If you are loathe to fill the air with pesticide sprays, try using a cardboard spike that has been impregnated with pesticide. The spike is pushed into the plant container and the pesticide moves into the soil and is taken up by the plant. When pests feed on the plant they are poisoned.

Types of pesticide

There are two types of pesticide. Systemic ones are taken up by the plant, while contact (non-systemic) pesticides are sprayed or dusted on to the plant and have to touch the pest to work.

Check the label to see which type you are buying. The label will also list the chemicals the pesticide contains, the pests it will kill and common plants it should not be used on.

Some plants are damaged by certain pesticides. Follow the maker's instructions carefully, especially when using pesticides on food crops.

Bees are very susceptible to pesticides, so if you must spray a plant in flower (which will be visited by bees and other pollinators), wait until evening when they have stopped flying. There is then plenty of time for the spray to settle before the morning.

How do you know what is attacking the plant? If you cannot find the creature, look

A CHOICE OF CHEMICALS

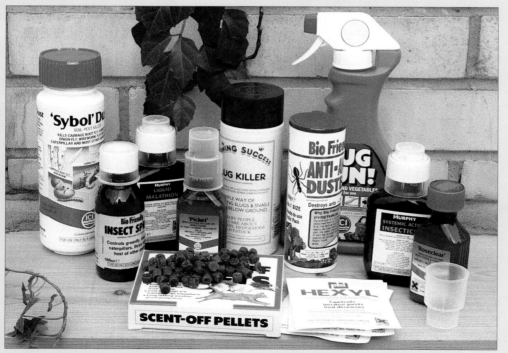

There is a wide variety of pesticides on the market and good stockists will have several alternative brands for whatever pest problem you may need to counter. Read the labels carefully before you buy and when using any insecticide.

Tom Deas

Capsid bugs suck the sap from young growths, deforming leaves, shoots and buds. They attack fruit trees such as apples (left), currant bushes and herbaceous ornamental plants. Fruit trees and bushes can be sprayed to kill overwintering eggs. In summer, frequent spraying can contain infestations on ornamental plants.

Leaf miners (right) leave tell-tale pale tunnels in the leaves they attack. This is chrysanthemum leaf miner. Outdoors, the problem occurs in late spring and summer, but under glass it can be continuous. Spray at the first sign of infestation.

Red spider mites (below right) attack plants indoors and in the greenhouse, and may attack herbaceous plants and shrubs in the garden. Adult mites can develop resistance to gamma-HCH, so it is best to use a variety of chemicals. Alternatively, try biological control by introducing the predatory mite Phytoseiulus persimilis (far right).

Peter McHoy

Peter McHoy

SYMPTOMS OF COMMON PESTS

Aphids (greenfly, blackfly): Leaves stunted or curled up. Lower leaves sticky with honeydew secreted by aphids. Sooty mould may grow on this, blackening the plant. Look for aphids on stem tips, buds and young leaves. May be winged or wingless.

Capsid bugs: Produce tattered leaves and also feed on flower buds so that emerging flower is very distorted.

Caterpillars: Small holes eaten out of leaves. Eventually whole leaf eaten except the veins. Look on underside and edge of leaf for culprit. It may have dropped off the plant to pupate by the time you notice the holes.

Eelworms: Distorted growth of stems and leaves of bulbous plants. Distorted growth, including blooms, of chrysanthemums.

Slugs or snails: Plant has ragged, irregular holes left by rasping mouth of slug or snail. Slime trail usually evident and culprit may be close by.

Spider mite: Leaves appear pale and speckled. On close inspection, very fine strands of web visible on leaf and stem.

Whitefly: Clouds of small white flies emerge from plant when it is tapped gently or moved.

at the damage for a clue. If the whole plant keels over and dies, suspect a root or stem eater or fungus disease. Have a look in the soil for grubs and go out at night with a torch to see if slugs are about. If you cannot find the culprit, it will have moved on, so there is no point in spraying.

Leaf-eaters

If leaves are bitten to produce a scalloped pattern, weevils are to blame. They can be controlled, if necessary, with malathion. Vine weevil damages roots and stems, especially in greenhouse pot plants. They can be controlled by careful hygiene and use of HCH.

If the leaves have cleanly cut holes, which eventually join up, suspect caterpillars of

Pat Brindley

moths or butterflies or the larval stage of sawfly. Pick off eggs and caterpillars and hoe beneath the plant to expose pupating stages to the birds. Derris is a useful contact pesticide, as are malathion and permethrin. After using any of these allow several days before harvesting any crop.

Sap-suckers

Sap-sucking pests weaken the plant, distort growth and can also spread viruses. Aphids (greenfly and blackfly) multiply fast and make plants sticky with their honeydew. Sooty moulds grow on the sugar and spoil the plant's appearance.

Use derris or malathion or the highly selective pirimicarb, which leaves predators alive. Where aphids are feeding in rolled up leaves, use the systemic dimethoate.

Capsid bugs produce tattered holes, killing buds and shoots and deforming emerging flowers. Remove leaf litter, in which they overwinter, from around the base of the plant.

In spring, summer and autumn, when the pests are active, spray with malathion or the systemic dimethoate. Check the label with regard to

PESTICIDE SAFETY

- Read the label before you buy the pesticide to ensure that it is the correct one for the pest and the plant.
- Read the instructions for protective clothing (usually gloves and perhaps goggles) and dose rate.
- Keep a sprayer or watering can for pesticide use only and mark it accordingly. Keep a measuring jug and mixing stick solely for this job too.
- Take water out to the sprayer in a bucket, don't bring the sprayer into the kitchen.
- Don't spray on a windy day and if the plant is in flower, wait until evening when the bees will have left.
- Observe harvest intervals on maker's instructions if spraying fruit or vegetables.

DON'T FORGET!

spraying at flowering times.

The leafhopper is the insect responsible for cuckoo-spit on plants. It does little damage and can be hosed off.

Red spider mite is a problem in greenhouses and on fruit

Peter McHoy

Peter McHoy

Plant spikes or plant pins (above), impregnated with insecticides, can be used with pot plants.

Young trees are particularly vulnerable to damage from rabbits and will need to be protected (below). Cats can also present the gardener with problems (facing page) and can be discouraged to some extent with strong-smelling animal repellents.

Photos Horticultural

outdoors. Leaves become pale and mottled and covered with fine cobwebs. Good greenhouse hygiene and spraying plants with water twice daily in summer, to keep the humidity level up, keeps red spider mite under control. Crowded, dry conditions encourage this pest. For pot plants, plant spikes impregnated with butoxycarboxim are effective.

Outdoors, chemical controls are poor, but fungicides such as benomyl have some effect.

Avoid using winter washes because these kill predators too, making the problem worse.

Rasping damage

Fly larvae in the soil can damage roots and stem bases; diazinon and bromophos are useful against soil pests. Leaf miners live between the upper and lower surfaces of leaves. They are particularly noticeable on holly and chrysanthemum, but also occur on other plants. Dimethoate controls them; pick off leaves that are badly infested.

Leatherjackets are the larvae of crane flies (daddy-long-legs). They live in the soil and damage roots of poorly maintained lawns and of plants in ground that was recently a lawn. Look after the lawn and cultivate soil for planting, so that birds can eat the larvae, to minimize damage.

Other pests

Wasps are not a plant pest but can be a nuisance in late summer when they are seeking sugar. A jam jar trap, containing water and jam, is useful for distracting them when you want to eat in the garden, but it will have little effect on the population. If you have a nest call in a pest control expert.

Bees may swarm and arrive in your garden, but they will do little harm if left alone.

Ants can be kept from the house by spreading crushed mothballs near the threshold and, if need be, you can buy ant-killer if they are still getting into food.

Worms producing casts on the lawn are a nuisance and can be discouraged by using acidic fertilizers (lawn sand is acidic). If you discourage worms, you will also discourage moles, because their principal food is worms.

Birds are useful in the garden but some species strip fruit buds and the fruit itself. A cage or netting is the answer. Grass seed is often treated with bird repellant so there is no need to worry about the birds when sowing a new lawn with such seed.

Mice and rats are best dealt with by a pest controller. It can be useful, though, to trap them to identify the species.

Rabbits, dogs and cats can be kept out by barriers (deep ones in the case of rabbits) and can be discouraged to some extent from fouling by using animal repellants – the stronger smelling the better.

Squirrels can be a problem. A fruit cage will keep them off your crop and spiral tree guards will stop them ringbarking woody plants. Burying bulbs in a wire mesh cage or with gorse cuttings will stop squirrels digging them up.

GARDEN NOTES

TYPES OF PESTICIDE

Contact:
Aluminium sulphate (for slugs and snails)
Carbaryl
Derris (rotenone)
Gamma-HCH
Horticultural soap
Malathion
Permethrin
Pirimicarb
Pirimiphos-methyl
Resmethrin
Ingested:
Metaldehyde (against slugs and snails)
Systemic:
Dimethoate

Dealing with
Plant Diseases

Diseases are hidden dangers to plants, often remaining undetected until infection is severe, but there are ways to prevent and control them.

There are three main types of diseases that attack plants – fungal, bacterial and viral. Some other problems are disease-like, but are caused by unsuitable environments and errors in cultivation. These types of setback are known as physiological disorders.

All of these problems have distinctive characteristics, and each requires separate treatments to control them.

Fungal diseases

There are numerous fungal diseases and some are widespread, including mildews and rusts. Once a fungus enters a plant, minute and thread-like growths, known as hyphae, spread throughout the stems, leaves and shoots.

The disease spreads from one plant to another by microscopic spores that develop on the plant's surface, sometimes entering through cuts and other damage. Once the spores germinate, the hyphae rapidly take over the plant.

Some fungal diseases attack a wide range of plants, while others restrict their attention to just one or a few hosts.

Bacterial diseases

The bacteria that cause disease are microscopic, single-celled organisms that develop within a plant and cause damage. They are not so easy to control as fungal diseases.

Bacterial infections enter plants through wounds, prun-

Fireblight (above) is a bacterial disease which affects trees and shrubs in the Rosaceae family. Here it has attacked the leaves of Sorbus sargentiana.

There are many different types of rust, some of which affect only certain species. All are caused by a fungal infection. Here (left) rust spots have affected the leaves of a Hypericum.

Most virus diseases are spread by tiny creatures such as greenfly (right).

Grey mould (below) is a fungal disease that can affect all plants. Spores spread easily.

sects previously in contact with contaminated plants. Activities such as removing side-shoots on tomato plants can increase the chance of infection because they open up a sappy wound to insects.

Once a plant is infected, nothing can be done to remove the virus. Avoid propagating from infected plants.

Greenfly (aphids) are the main cause of a virus spreading and it is, therefore, vital that insect pests are controlled by regularly spraying plants.

Viruses seldom kill plants. Indeed, if they did, the virus would not have a host. Rather, they cause loss of vigour and a general lack of well being.

In a commercial situation, with the aid of science, the shoot tips of infected plants can be encouraged to grow rapidly and produce virus-free cuttings. A home gardener,

ing cuts, natural cracks in stems and damage to leaves. Moisture is vital to bacteria and therefore infection is worse during wet weather, especially when it is warm.

Examples of bacterial diseases include gladiolus scab and crown gall, a disease that attacks a wide range of plants, from gladioli to brambles, creating wart-like growths.

Virulent viruses

A virus is a living organism, so small that it can only be seen with the aid of an electron microscope. Therefore, it is only the effect of a virus that is seen, not the cause.

Viruses are often introduced into the sap of plants by in-

PLANTS AT RISK

Warmth and high humidity, coupled with soft stems, leaves and fruits, are a dangerous combination when disease spores are about.

Do not . . .

• excessively feed plants with nitrogen, or they will produce soft, floppy stems and leaves.

• set plants too close together, as this will prevent the circulation of air around them. Moist, stagnant air in confined places encourages diseases.

• create a stuffy, warm atmosphere in greenhouses and conservatories. And avoid cold winds blowing on plants in winter. Always open the ventilator on the lee side.

• damage plants and fruits, as this quickly allows disease spores to enter. Apples and pears soon become infected if roughly handled.

• leave infected fruits on plants – destroy them immediately.

• neglect treating diseases. The earlier plants are dusted or sprayed, the better the chance of recovery – it also prevents the disease from spreading further.

SYSTEMIC FUNGICIDES

The best way to control diseases is to spray before an attack and then to give further treatments at regular intervals. As with insecticides, there are also systemic fungicides. They enter a plant's tissue and remain active against diseases for several weeks.

The chemical **carbendazim**, for instance, is a systemic fungicide for the control of a wide range of diseases of flowering plants, bulbs, shrubs, vegetables and fruit. The chemicals **bupirimate** and **triforine** can also be used to control diseases on flowering plants, shrubs, roses and fruit, controlling black spot on roses, powdery mildew and apple scab.

GARDEN NOTES

however, has no choice but to remove and burn infected plants. Try also to ensure that infection is not taken into your garden on infected plants.

Occasionally, plants with viruses are specially selected because of the attractive mottling and coloration that viruses can produce.

The multi-colouring and streaking in some tulips is sometimes caused by viruses. So, too, is the attractive mottling on spotted flowering maple, *Abutilon striatum* 'Thompsonii'. This widely grown houseplant is also often used in summer-bedding displays.

Physiological disorders

Plant disorders brought about by environmental factors and incorrect cultivation are not contagious. One such example is the practice of spraying soft leaves with water when they are in strong sunlight; the water droplets act as lenses, causing the tissue to burn.

Fruits that are roughly

Tulips with broken colours, such as the two burgundy and white ones (above left), are popular. The colours are often caused by a virus. Rembrandt tulips are old varieties of this type.

A good chemical sprayer (top) will focus your fungicide where it is needed.

Immersing cuttings in a fungicide (above) before planting them will protect them at a vulnerable time.

Apple scab (left) damages fruit, leaves and the young shoots of apple trees. It is a fungal disease which can be particularly bad after a wet spring.

handled when being picked will, when stored, develop bruises that encourage the entry of storage rots.

Plants can also be damaged through being given too little or too much nutrient. Lack of water will also cause damage.

Badly drained soil prevents plants growing properly, as they require a healthy balance between moisture and air around their roots.

Garden husbandry

Whenever a plant disease – or pest – is mentioned, the first reaction is to ask, 'What can I spray it with?' But usually this is not the only solution. Good garden husbandry is actually just as important.

SOME COMMON DISEASES

Name	Description	Control
American gooseberry mildew	Attacks leaves, shoots and fruits of gooseberries, creating a white powdery coating that changes to pale brown. If not controlled, bushes eventually die. Blackcurrants are also infected, but late in the season.	Spray with benomyl or thiophanate-methyl in spring and repeat at two-week intervals. A good air circulation around plants reduces infection. Do not over-feed plants with nitrogen, as this encourages lush shoots that are liable to infection.
Apple canker	Attacks both apples and pears, entering through damage caused by pests. Sunken patches that resemble small oyster shells form around damaged areas, spreading and girdling limbs. Young shoots die.	Cut out and burn infected shoots and branches. Cover large pruning cuts with a fungicidal paint. Regular spraying against insects prevents them causing damage through which the disease gains access.
Apple mildew	Creates a white, powdery coating on leaves and shoots of apples, pears, crab apples, medlars and quinces. 'Cox's Orange Pippin' is an apple variety that is especially susceptible.	Remove and burn seriously infected shoots and spray with benomyl or thiophanate-methyl at the pink bud stage in late spring, repeating the spray every 10-14 days until midsummer.
Apple scab	Attacks apples and other members of the *Malus* family. Creates matt, green-black spots on leaves and fruits, often causing them to split.	Fungus overwinters on fallen leaves, so collect and burn them. Spray trees with benomyl or thiophanate-methyl.
Bacterial canker	Attacks plums, peaches, cherries and ornamental *Prunus* trees, especially young ones. Cankers form and shoots slowly die.	Disease enters branches through cuts. Therefore, only prune these trees in summer, when the sap is rising. Coat all pruning cuts with a bacterial wound paint.
Black leg	Mainly attacks cuttings, especially pelargoniums, causing the bases of stems to become soft and black.	Infection is encouraged by wet, cold, air-less and compacted potting compost. Remove and destroy seriously infected cuttings, but those slightly damaged can be saved by cutting away black areas and re-potting in clean compost.
Black spot	Common on roses and first seen on young leaves in spring, developing from overwintering spores. Slowly, the black spots spread and merge. Infected leaves fall off prematurely.	Remove and burn infected leaves, as well as all shoots removed during pruning. Immediately after pruning, spray with or thiophanate-methyl every two or three weeks until late summer.
Brown rot	Infects insect-damaged fruits, creating concentric rings of raised spores. Fruits that have been roughly picked often begin to rot later.	Spray trees regularly and avoid damaging fruits when they are picked. Check stored fruits and remove infected ones.
Clematis wilt	Results in wilting and die-back in clematis, especially with large-flowered varieties of *Clematis* × *jackmanii.* Plants suddenly wilt, but are rarely killed. Fresh shoots develop below infected areas or grow up from the ground.	Cut out infected shoots. In spring, spray with Bordeaux mixture.

See the next page for details of more diseases.

Powdery mildew can affect the leaves and stems of a rose (left), and also the buds. Many different mildews attack a wide variety of plants, though some are specific to certain hosts. Remove and burn all diseased growth, especially in autumn to prevent the fungus overwintering. If need be, spray in spring and summer.

S & O Mathews

Name	Description	Control
Damping off	Widely damaging to seedlings in seed boxes in greenhouses. Overcrowded seedlings in very wet, unsterilized and compacted potting compost collapse and die. High temperatures encourage this disease.	Ensure compost is sterilized. Also, wash seed trays and boxes. Attacks can be checked by watering the compost with Cheshunt compound.
Fireblight	Affects pears and apples, as well as ornamental trees and shrubs such as *Cotoneaster* and *Crataegus*. Fruit spurs are attacked, leaves shrivel and turn brown, then black.	All infections in England and Wales must be notified to the Ministry of Agriculture. Cut out and burn infected shoots, 90cm/3ft below the infection.
Grey mould (also known as botrytis)	Infection enters plants through wounds and cuts. Grey, fluffy spores appear in clusters. They spread rapidly in wet weather, covering soft leaves, petals and fruits.	Remove and burn infected parts. Avoid excessive watering and ensure plants in greenhouses are well ventilated. Sterilize the potting compost and containers, and spray with benomyl or thiophanate-methyl.
Peach leaf curl	Mainly attacks peach trees, but also seen on apricots, almonds, nectarines and ornamental cherries. In early spring, young leaves assume a crimson flush, then thicken, curl and crumple. They become covered in a white bloom and soon fall off the tree.	Pick up and burn all fallen leaves. Spray trees in spring with Bordeaux mixture, repeating two weeks later. Additionally, spray trees when the leaves start to fall.
Rose mildew	Infects roses, especially in wet weather and when days are warm and nights cold. Small grey or white spots appear, spreading to form a felt-like grey down. Also, shoot tips are killed and buds fail to open.	Do not plant rose bushes close together – they need good air circulation around them. Spray infected leaves thoroughly with a copper-based fungicide or with bupirimate with triforine.
Rusts	Complex diseases. Many types, with varied life styles and range of hosts. Brown or black spots develop into irregular, raised blotches. Makes plants unsightly and impairs growth.	Difficult to control. Burn seriously infected plants, reduce humidity and ventilate freely. Soft stems and leaves encourage rusts. Spray with mancozeb or propiconazole, or with myclobutanil for rose rust.
Tulip fire	Encouraged by wet, cold weather in early spring. Infection first appears as deformed shoots and leaves, revealing small, sunken, grey spots that spread to form patches. Fungal spores live in the soil for several years.	Carefully remove infected plants and immediately burn. In spring, spray with benomyl when shoots are 5cm/2in high. Repeat the spraying at 10-day intervals until plants start flowering.

Removing and burning infected plants is vital. For instance, rose leaves infected with black spot – as well as shoots that have been cut off during pruning – should be burned immediately. The spores of apple scab over-winter on leaves and shoots, and these should be burned to stop it spreading.

Rotate plants throughout the garden from year to year. This particularly helps to prevent the build up of plant problems in vegetable plots.

Good stock

Only buy plants from reliable sources that claim to sell disease-free plants. Virus-free strawberry plants, for instance, can be bought from specialist nurseries. And remember that insects transmit diseases, so ensure that plants are free of these.

The grey film covering the strawberries (facing page) is characteristic of grey mould or botrytis.

A CLEAN START

Preventing infection is essential. Once a disease is established, eradication is difficult.

For instance, the notorious club root disease in cabbages and other plants in the brassica family (including wallflowers and stocks) can be controlled by dipping the roots of young plants – when they are being planted – in a fungicidal paste.

Alternatively, plants newly transplanted can be watered with a fungicide.

Additionally, dusting the seed drills of many vegetables with a combined disease and pest dressing helps to prevent the onset of diseases and pests. Importantly, it reduces the chance of diseases entering seedlings through damage caused by insects.

GARDEN NOTES

Index

Page numbers in *italic* refer to illustrations

A

Abutilon striatum
'Thompsonii' 90
Acanthus spinosus 66
Acer negundo 'Flamingo' 14
A. pseudoplatanus
'Brilliantissimum' 14
Achillea ptarmica 'The Pearl'
59, *59*, 60
acid soil 72, 73, 81
Agapanthus 54
ageratum 68, *68*
Ajuga reptans 'Burgundy
Glow' 65, 67
Alchemilla mollis 51
allium 52, 65, 66
A. albopilosum 66
A. cernuum 66
A. giganteum 66
A. rosenbachianum 65
A. siculum 66
alpines 22
alyssum 50, 68
A. maritima 'Little Dorrit' 60
A. saxatile 55
Amelanchier lamarckii 14
Anaphalis margaritacea 59, 60
Anemone x *hybrida*
(Japanese) 52, 66
animal pests 86
annuals *51*, 60, 65, 68
ants 86
aphids 85, 89, *89*
apple 50-1, *90*, 91, 93
aquilegia *49*, 50, 51
archangel 56
arches 50
architectural garden 19
Artemisia 63
A. ludoviciana 66
A. l. albula 58, 60, 61
'Powis Castle' *35*
artichoke, globe 51
autumn crocus 62, 65, 66
azalea 65, 67

B

bacterial diseases 88-9
bark 16, 71, 73
bay 34, 35, 39
beans 51
bear's breeches 66
bedding plants 31, 57
beds 10, 14-15, 21, 30-1
beech *15*

bees *52*, 83, 86
begonia 31, 57
B. semperflorens 34
'Silver Devil' *35*
bilboquet 41
birdbath *31*, 39
birds 61, 86
black leg 91
black spot 91, 93
blue plants 53-7
bluebell 56
boggy areas 24
bone meal *78*
borders 10, *12*, 14-15, *51*, 52
boundaries 7, 12, 13-14, 20
box 16, 33, 35, *37*, 39, 43, *43*,
45
dwarf 16, *38*, 40, 51
bracken 71
broom *10*, 55
dwarf 13
weeping 13
brown rot 91
buddleia *9*, 10, 61
B. alternifolia 14
B. davidii 61
bugle 56, 65, 67
buildings, garden 16
bulbs 41, 52, 62, 65-6
busy Lizzie 51, 68
buttercup, meadow 56
butterfly bush *see* buddleia
Buxus sempervirens 35, 43, *43*
'Suffruticosa' 33, *38*, 40

C

cabbage palm 31
calcium 71, 79
California lilac 54, *55*, 67, *67*
camassia 62
camellia 65, 67, 81
campanula 50, *51*
campion *50*
candytuft 68
canker 91
capsid bugs *84*, 85
carnation 37
caterpillars 84
catmint *49*, 65, 68
Ceanothus 54, *65*, 67
C. impressus 55
C. x *veitchianus 67*
cedar, western red 35
celandine, lesser 56
Centaurea cyanus 56
Centranthus 50
Cerastium tomentosum 61
Ceratostigma willmottianum
13, *13*

Cercis siliquastrum 14
Chaenomeles 13
Chamaecyparis lawsoniana 35
cherry 63
Chionodoxa 54
C. sardensis 54
chrysanthemum *50*, *55*, 57, 86
C. segetum 56
cinquefoil, shrubby 55
Cistus 13
citrus tree 35
clay soil 26, 71, 74
clematis 22, 50, 51, 67
C. armandii 63
C. flammula 63
'Henryi' *62*, 63
C. montana 22, 67
'Nelly Moser' 67
'Proteus' 67
clematis wilt 91
Cleome spinosa 65, 68
'Colour Fountain' 68
climbers 50, *51*, 63, 67
clothes drying area 10
club root disease 93
Colchicum autumnale 66
C. speciosum 'Album' 62
colour schemes
blue & yellow 53-7
pastels 64-9
white 58-63
columbine 50
compost 70-7
concrete, cracked 22
containers 16, *27*, 34, *43*, 44,
45, 61, 67, *86*
ageing 32
Convolvulus cneorum 61
Cordyline australis 31
Coreopsis lanceolata 57
cornflower *50*, 51, 56
Cornus controversa
'Variegata' 63
Cosmea (cosmos) *50*
C. bipinnatus 68
cottage garden 19, 48-52
cotton lavender *37*, 40
courtyard garden 19
crab apple 14
cranesbill *50*, 51, 52, *57*
crocus 41
C. sieberi 62
crown gall 89
crown imperial 31
curves 7, 19, 20
Cyclamen coum 62
cypress, Lawson's 35
Cytisus battandieri 55
C. kewensis 13

D

daffodil 41
dahlia *61*
daisy bush 61
damping off 93
Daphne mezereum 13
dead-heading 59
decking *19*
delphinium *49*, 50, 51, 52, 54,
54, 56, 57, *57*
Belladonna hybrids 66
design principles 7, 19
Deutzia 65
D. longifolia 'Veitchii' *67*, *67*
Dianthus 51
D. allwoodii 67
'Mrs Sinkins' 60, *60*
diascia *63*
digging *71*, 72
Digitalis purpurea 'Alba' 59, 60
diseases 88-93
dividing garden 7, 20, 21-2
Dorycnium hirsutum 61, *62*
drainage 71, *71*

E

Echinops 51
edging plants *51*, 61, 65, 67
Eranthis hyemalis 54, *55*
established garden 11
euphorbia *57*
evening primrose 55
evergreens 13, 43
everlasting pearl 59, 60

F

farmyard manure 72, *72*, 74,
79
Fatsia japonica 34
fences 10, 13, 20
fertilizers 78-81
fireblight *89*, 93
flax, perennial 66, *66*
focal points 7, *7*, 19, *33*
foliage, silver 58-63, 65, 66
foliar feeds 81, *81*
forget-me-not 30, 40, 50, 51,
54, 56, *64*, 65
formal garden 16, 19, 30-5
Forsythia x *intermedia* 55
'Spectabilis' *53*
fountain 39
foxglove 50, 51, 59, 60
fragrance *51*, 52
Fritillaria imperialis 31
fruit 7, 15, 50-1, *90*, 91, 93
fuchsia, hardy 13

fungal diseases 88
fungicides 90-3

G

garage, screening 11, 22
garden compost 72, *72*, 74-7, 79
Genista hispanica 10
   G. lydia 13
geometric shapes 34, 44
geranium 51
gladiolus *52*, 62
Gleditsia triacanthos
   'Sunburst' 14
glory of the snow 54, *54*
gold dust 55
golden rod *54*, 55
gooseberry mildew 91
gorse, Spanish *10*
grape hyacinth *54*, 62
grass cuttings 75, 79
gravel *45*, 73
   areas 9, 10, *11*, 21, *33*
   knot garden 37, 38, *38*
   paths 13
green manuring 70, *70*
greenhouse 10, 13, 82, 84, 85-6
grey foliage 58-63
grey mould *89*, 93
ground cover 21
Gypsophila paniculata 58
   'Bristol Fairy' *59*, 60

H

Hamamelis mollis 51, 55
hay 73
heather 13, 81
Hebe 13
Hedera helix 46
hedge 7, 12, 14, *15*, 16
   formal 33, 35
   knot garden *37*, 38, 40
   topiary 47
Helianthemum 13
Helichrysum petiolare 34, 61, *61*, 66
Helleborus 50
herbaceous plants 13
herbs 31, 33, 37, 41, 51, *51*
   garden 16, *41*
Hibiscus syriacus 13, *16*
hidden areas 7
hoeing 73
holly 35, 63, 86
   hedgehog 44
hollyhock 51, 65, 68
honesty 51
honeysuckle 22, 50, 52
   Chinese 44, *44*, 45, 47
hops 73
hyacinth 41, *56*
hydrangea 13, 16, 61
   H. paniculata 60
Hypericum 88
Hyssopus officinalis (hyssop) 40

I

Ilex aquifolium 35
   'Ferox' 44
   'Silver Queen' 63
inorganic fertilizer 79, 80
Ipheion uniflorum 61, 65
   'Caeruleum' *65*
iris 52, *57*
iron 79
island beds 21
ivy 46-7, 61
   Boston *22*

J

Japanese garden 19
jasmine, winter 50
Judas tree 14, *14*

K

knot garden 37-41

L

Laburnum 'Vossii' 14
lamb's ears 51, 66, *66*
Lamium galeobdolon 56
landscaping 18-23
laurel 11
Lavandula (lavender) 16, *37*, 51, 52
   'Munstead' 40
   L. vera (Dutch l.) 31
Lavatera 50, 51, 65
   L. olbia 'Rosea' *64*, 67
   L. thuringiaca 64
lawn 7, *7*, 9, 13, 20, 21, 23, *29*, 44
   fertilizer *79*, 80, 81, *81*
   from seed 24-9
   from turf 10, 29
   improving 31
   mowing 21, 27
   raised *21*
   reseeding 25
leaf-eating pests 84-5
leafhopper 85
leaf miner *84*, 86
leaf mould 73, *73*
leatherjackets 86
levels 20, 23, 32
Ligustrum ovalifolium 43, 44, 47
   L. vulgare 'Aureum' 43
lilac 51, 61
lily 51, 52, 62
   African 54
   day 56
   Madonna 62
lily of the valley 65, 66
lime 26, 72, 73, *81*
Linaria 50
   L. vulgaris 56
Linum narbonense 66, *66*
liquid fertilizer 81
lobelia 61
   L. erinus 54

London pride 51
long narrow garden 7, *20*, 21
Lonicera nitida 'Baggesen's Gold' 44, 47
love-in-a-mist 57, 68
low-maintenance garden 21
lupin *51*, 52
Lychnis coronaria 'Alba' 59, 60

M

magnesium 79
mallow 50, 51
   tree *64*, 65, 67
Malus 14
manure 70, 72, *72*, 79-80, *80*
maple, spotted flowering 90
marigold 56
   African 57
   corn 56
   French 40, 57
   pot 50
Matthiola 'Giant Imperial' 60
measuring site 7, 21
mice 86
Michaelmas daisy 52
micro-organisms, soil 71, 74
mildew 88, 91, 93, *93*
minute garden 22
mock orange 61
Morus nigra 14
mulberry 14
mulching 72, 73, 75
mushroom compost 73
Myosotis 50, 54

N

narcissus 62
nasturtium 40
Nepeta 58
   N. mussinii 65, 68
nerine 65, 66
   N. bowdenii 'Pink Triumph' 66
New Zealand flax 34
nicotiana 51, 52
nitrogen 79, 81
nutrients 79

O

Oenothera 55
Olearia mollis 61
   O. virgata 61
onion, ornamental *65*, 66
organic gardening 77, 80, 82
ornamental garden 30-5
outbuildings, disguising 22, *22*
overgrown sites 15

P

palm 34
pansy *31*, 37, 40, *50*, 54, *56-7*, 61, 68
Papaver 50
parterre 33, *39*

Parthenocissus tricuspidata 22
pastel schemes 64-9
paths 10, 12, 13, *13*, 20, 21, 22, *23*
patio 9, 10, *12*, 13, *13-14*, 23, 46
paved garden 19
paving slabs 13, *20*, *33*
peach leaf curl 93
pear, weeping 63
peas 51
peat 73, 79
pelargonium 31, 40, 61
peony *51*
perennials *51*, 60
pergola 10, 11, 13
periwinkle 54
Pernettya mucronata 13
Perovskia atriplicifolia 13, 65, 67
pests & pesticides 82-6
petunia 40, 51, 61
pH test 26, 72
Philadelphus 61
Phormium 34
phosphorus 78
physiological disorders 88, 90-1
pinks 37, 40, 51, *60*, 65, 67
planning 6-16
planting 10, 12
play area 16
plumbago, hardy 13
polyanthus 30, 40
Polygonum baldschuanicum 61
pond 10, 13, 15, 21, 23, 32, 34, *35*
poplar 16
poppy 50, 51
   Californian 57
potassium 78
Potentilla 55
potting compost 72
powdery mildew *93*
primrose 56
privacy 20
privet 43, 45, 47
Prunus 63
   P. avium 'Plena' 63
pyracantha 10
Pyrus salicifolia 'Pendula' 63

Q

quince, ornamental 13

R

rabbits *86*
railway sleepers *23*
Ranunculus acris 56
rats 86
rectangular garden 7, *10*, 21
red spider mite *84*, 85-6
rhododendron 11, 65, 67, 81
Ribes sanguineum 51
rock garden 10, 23, 67
rock rose 13
Rosa (rose) 11, 13, 33, 61, 63, 82, 93, *93*

climbing 50, 51
floribunda 33
hybrid tea 13, 33
'Iceberg' *58*, 61, *61*
miniature 33, *50*
old-fashioned 48-50, 52
standard 31, 33, 34, 39
rose campion 59
roundwork 41
rust 88, *88*, 93

S

safety 23, 85
sage, flowering 65, 68
purple-leaved *41*
Russian 13, 65, 67
salvia 51, 52, *57*
S. horminum 65, 68
sand 26, 73
sandpit 10, 16, *21*
sandy soil 71, *72*, 74
Santolina chamaecyparissus
40
sap-sucking pests 85
sawdust 73
sawfly *83*, 85
scale plan 6, 8, *18-19*, 21, 38
scented garden 22
scilla 56
scree bed 15, *15*
screens 7, 13-14, *14*, 16
seaweed 73
Sedum 'Autumn Joy' *66*
seed compost 72
self-seeders 50, *51*
Senecio bicolor 31
S. maritima 60, 61, 65
Sequestrene 81

shade 9-10, 23, 24
shrubs 11, 13, *16*, *51*
fast-growing 10, 13
pastel 65, 67
white-flowered 61, 63
silts 71
silver foliage 58-63, 65, *66*
slopes 23
slugs 84
snapdragon 56, 57
snowdrop 62
snow-in-cement 61
snowy mespilus 14
soil
improving 26, 70-3
pests 86
test kit 26, 72, 80
Solidago 55
Sorbus sargentiana 89
speedwell, germander 56
spider flower 65, 68, *68*
sprinkler system 71
squirrels 86
Stachys lanata 51, *66*
star flower, spring 62, 65, *65*
statues *11*, 33-4, *33*, 39
stepping stones *11*, 13
steps *22*, 23
stock, night-scented 51, 52
Strantia 51
straw 73
styles of garden 19
sun 9-10
sundial 34
sunken garden 31-3
sweet pea *50*
sweet William *49*, *50*, *51*
symmetry 30, 32, 37

T

Tagetes 'Yellow Gem' *35*
Taxus baccata 35, 43
terracing 23
textures 20
theme garden 13
Thuja plicata 'Atrovirens' 35
thyme 22, 51
tickseed *57*
toadflax 56
tobacco plant 51, 52, 57
tomato fertilizer 80
top dressing 81
topiary 16, 35, 43-7
Trachycarpus fortunei 34
trees 20, 22, 23, 38, 63
for small gardens 14, 15-16
planting 13
removing 15
trellis 7, 20, *20*
screens 13-14, *14*
trench, for compost 76-7
Tudor knot 40
tulip fire 93
Tulipa (tulip) 30, 37, 41, *56*,
62, *64*, 65, 90, *90*
T. fosteriana 'Candela' *54*
'Pax' *31*
'Rembrandt' *90*

U

urns *11*, *30*, *33*, 34

V

valerian, white *58*
vegetables 7-9, *9*, 15, 51, 70, 75

Veronica chamaedrys 56
viburnum 61
V. fragrans 51
Vinca 54
vine, Russian 22, *61*
vine weevil 84
Viola 54
violet, sweet 40
viruses 89-90

W

wallflower 30, 50
walls 10, 12, 13, *13*, 22
wasps 86
water features *21*
wedding cake tree 63
weeds 15, 21, 25, 26
weevil *83*, 84
white schemes 58-63
wild flowers *51*, *52*, 56
wild garden 16
willow 16
winter aconite 55, *55*
wire formers 46
Wisteria floribunda 'Alba' 63,
63
W. sinensis 'Alba' 63
witch hazel 51, 55
woodland garden 19
worms 71, 86

Y

yard garden *19*, 22
yellow plants 53-7
yew 11, 16, 35, 43, 45
yucca 34

*P*hotogra*p*hic *C*redits

ANDREW LAWSON *15, 20, 30, 34, 39, 41, 44, 45, 46, 56, 64, 75, 90*
COLLECTIONS *31, 70, 72, 80, 81*
DAVID SQUIRE *17, 54, 55*; DEREK GOULD *16, 54, 62*; DON WILDRIDGE *7, 83*
ERIC CRICHTON *9, 26, 38, 41, 45, 50, 57, 67, 70, 73, 77, 78, 90*
GARDEN PICTURE LIBRARY *6, 9, 11, 14, 18, 19, 20, 21, 22, 25, 37, 47, 51, 52, 55, 56, 59, 62, 65, 90*
GILLIAN BECKETT *53, 61, 63*; HARRY SMITH COLLECTION *12, 34, 35, 46, 52, 58, 66, 89*
INSIGHT PICTURE LIBRARY *49*; JONATHAN ALDEN *50*
MARSHALL CAVENDISH *25, 32, 72, 73, 74, 75, 78*
METRO PRODUCTS LTD, OXTED *76*
NEIL HOLMES *9, 10, 60, 88*
PAT BRINDLEY *11, 33, 65, 79, 80, 85*
PETER MCHOY *13, 25, 26, 28, 29, 31, 33, 36, 42, 43, 68, 69, 71, 77, 83, 84, 85, 86, 87, 90, 93*
PHOTOS HORTICULTURAL *13, 14, 15, 22, 23, 24, 27, 28, 44, 54, 55, 59, 60, 62, 67, 76, 86, 89*
RAY DUNS *46, 47*; S & O MATHEWS *58, 61, 64, 66, 92*
STEPHEN DALTON/NHPA *89*; TANIA MIDGLEY *39*; TOM DEAS *83*